# Political Crumbs

# Political Crumbs

HANS MAGNUS ENZENSBERGER

Translated by
Martin Chalmers

VERSO

London · New York

First published as *Politische Brosamen* by Suhrkamp Verlag, 1982
This edition published by Verso 1990
© Verso 1990
Translation © Verso 1990

**Verso**
UK: 6 Meard Street, London W1V 3HR
USA: 29 West 35th Street, New York, NY 10001-2291

Verso is the imprint of New Left Books

**British Library Cataloguing in Publication Data**

Enzensberger, Hans Magnus
Political crumbs.
1. Germany. Politics
I. Title   II. Politische Brosamen. *English*
320.943

ISBN 0-86091-294-9
ISBN 0-86091-512-3 pbk

**US Library of Congress Cataloging-in-Publication Data**

Enzensberger, Hans Magnus.
[Politische Brosamen. English]
Political crumbs / Hans Magnus Enzensberger : translated by Martin
Chalmers.
p.   cm.
Translation of: Politische Brosamen.
ISBN 0-86091-294-9. — ISBN 0-86091-512-3 (pbk.)
1. Germany (West)—Politics and government.   2. Political culture—
Germany (West)   3. Democracy.   4. Title
JN3971.A2E5913   1990
943.087'8—dc20

Typeset by Leaper & Gard Ltd, Bristol
Printed in the United States

# Contents

Note on Translations     vii

1   Second Thoughts on Consistency     1

2   Reluctant Eurocentrism: A Political Picture Puzzle     17

3   The Highest Stage of Underdevelopment: A Hypothesis about Really Existing Socialism     35

4   A Determined Effort to Explain to a New York Audience the Secrets of German Democracy     53

5   Ungovernability: Notes from the Chancellor's Office     71

6   Blind-Man's-Buff Economics     85

7   A Plea for the Home Tutor: A Little Bit of Educational Policy     97

8   Poor Little Rich Germany! Preliminary Sketches for a Study of Manners     111

9   On the Irresistibility of the Petty Bourgeoisie: A Sociological Caprice     125

10   In Defence of Normality     135

11   Two Notes on the End of the World     151

# Note on Translations

All translations are by Martin Chalmers, and published in English for the first time, except: Chapter 1, which was originally a lecture given in English at New York University's Center for the Humanities, and is revised for this book by Martin Chalmers; Chapter 4, first published in *New Left Review* 118, November–December 1979; Chapter 9, translated by David J. Parent and first published in *Telos* 30, Winter 1976; and Chapter 11, translated by David Fernbach and first published in *New Left Review* 110, July–August 1978. Permission to use these translations is gratefully acknowledged.

# 1

# Second Thoughts on Consistency

Once upon a time there was a black American revolutionary by
the name of Eldridge Cleaver. He spent some years in jail, wrote
a few books, became a Black Panther, went into exile, attempted
a comeback as a revolutionary designer of men's trousers, and
has not been heard of since. During the 1960s, however, Cleaver
coined a memorable phrase. 'Baby,' he said, 'you're either part
of the problem, or you're part of the solution.'

To many people and for a not inconsiderable period of time,
this seemed an apt maxim. Clearcut, unequivocal, uncompromising, it had the deceptively simple sound of a quotation from the
Bible. For some years afterwards, it was adopted by politically
minded people, not only in the USA, but also in Europe and in
what is sometimes called rather sweepingly the Third World.
The only trouble with Cleaver's handy dictum is that it does not
happen to be true. First of all, the solution is nowhere in sight.
There does not seem to be such a thing. Of course, there is a
huge supply of quick fixes – zillions of little remedies are being
offered by bodies as diverse as IBM, EST and the KGB – but
even their promoters would hardly claim they merit the majestic
singular of Cleaver's phrase.

More importantly, however, it has become very clear that
everybody is 'part of the problem'. Supposing, for the sake of
argument, that one was able to identify the 'good' side in any or
all of the many conflicts which beset the world and granted that
one would be willing to *take* it, this would in no way entitle one to

a feeling of justification, since one would inevitably continue to participate in the web of situations, arrangements and traditions which are, precisely, 'part of the problem'. In stating this rather obvious fact, I do not wish to imply that the 'baddies' cannot any longer be identified. On the contrary, this is fantastically easy. What I find nearly impossible is the opposite operation. To point out a 'goody' does not any longer seem feasible, least of all if a mirror is used.

This is a very disagreeable state of affairs, especially for concerned intellectuals, who for a century or two have thrived on basic tenets like the following: It is good and necessary to establish first principles. It is difficult but laudable to hang on to them at any cost. Compromise in the face of adversity, cutbacks and reaction is bad. A radical should be radical. Opportunism is sinful. Consistency is good.

I should like to think, though I cannot be sure, that these rules were laid down in simpler and harder times than ours. A man who was a devoted socialist in 1912, for example, was certain to be faced with difficulties but he could hardly be blamed if he thought of himself as 'part of the solution'. The same may be said of a Spanish anarchist of the 1930s, or of a Kibbutznik starting a new life in Palestine. A few of these men and women are still alive, and if you meet them you will find that they inspire a feeling close to awe. Unfortunately, their deep conviction has been inherited by a much lesser breed. Since the early sixties, a peculiar type of intransigent has made his appearance, a type who is very much a part of our problem, since he is uncommonly close to ourselves, our work, our milieu and our private lives. He is easy to recognize, but difficult to define, since he comes in a great number of varieties. I cannot be sure about America, but in Europe we have seen them all: the stern critic of monopoly state capitalism tucked away safely in a state-run university with tenure for life; the slave of intellectual fashion coming out strongly against intellectual fashion and its followers; the well-endowed bureaucrat of culture with a nauseating fondness for 'subversive' artists; the peace research fund director bullying his elegant female office staff, and so on. Needless to say, all these people are full of principles. Indeed the hazier their identity, the keener they are on the rhetoric of commitment. They all cherish a radical stance, untarnished by considerations arising out of their everyday existence.

Now it might be thought that there is nothing new in all this. The hypocrite and the pharisee are, after all, well-established and ancient types in the comedy of manners. And indeed, if this were just another instance of self-righteousness and of double standards of morality, we should be confronted with a cast of characters quite familiar from an Ibsen play. The point, however, is precisely that we are not dealing with individual characters or with a subjective deficiency, but rather with an absence of character and with an epidemic of objective proportions. The people I have in mind do not embrace principles because they believe in their inherent truth. They use them as a blunt instrument with which to bludgeon others. Principles are needed only for the purpose of defining others as opportunists, careerists, sellouts; moral, political or aesthetic renegades. The only person beyond suspicion is the one who has got hold of the microphone and who represents, at the moment of speaking, a higher reality of which, alas, he himself is not a part.

It is hard to identify this sheriff of conviction, this watchdog of basic values, this guru of principle. Indeed, it may turn out to be impossible. Speaking about him involves a moral paradox; this is a phenomenon which one risks becoming a part of the moment one speaks about it. No amount of sincerity will save one from the condition of moral schizophrenia which has become a universal of our intellectual existence. The very claim to a state of superior ethical grace is self-defeating.

Not many people are prepared to resign themselves to such a state of profound and permanent moral ambiguity. There is a heavy demand for idols who refuse to be part of the general quagmire, and a supply-side economy will not fail to provide what is needed. This is why we find, in our cultural marketplace, an unlikely assembly of cult figures who are supposed to be beyond suspicion. What they do for a living is of secondary importance. They may be philosophers or therapists, mystics or ideologues, artists or criminals, gurus or terrorists. The main demand made upon them is that they be part of the solution, not of the problem; that an unquestioned integrity can be ascribed to them; that they be untainted by doubt, compromise and equivocation. The result of this search is a curious Hall of Fame, a Madame Tussaud's of postmodern morality, crowded with figures such as Sid Vicious and Mother Teresa, Castaneda and Einstein, Samuel Beckett and Josef Stalin, Charles Manson and Erich Fromm, John Cage and Henry Abbot, Jian Qing and William S. Burroughs, Karel Woytila and Ulrike Meinhof, the Reverend Moon and Professor Beuys.

What is it, then, that we are so keen on that we want to acquire it at almost any cost, even if it means looking foolish or crazy, or obscene? It must be something utterly lost. I believe that this something is consistency, the notion that there ought to be a large degree of congruence or at least compatibility between what we are, what we think and what we do. Consistency is not a simple concept, and I am not sure of its status in Anglo-American philosophy. German philosophy, however, has traditionally been very strong on this notion, for which German philosophers have developed the term *Konsequenz*. This is, first of all, a logical category. In any rational discourse, judgements were supposed to follow from certain assumptions or first principles. In other words, one should not simply jump to conclusions or defend any old phrase which happened to pass through one's head as if it were a valid proposition. Contradictions would have to be avoided, overcome or at least explained. Very soon, and rather imperceptibly, this rule acquired moral overtones, and finally it became a postulate, an ethical imperative, and even something of an obsession, at least in Germany.

Mine is a culture which historically has been prone to believe that to possess principles and to act them out to their utmost consequences is good. Possibly this has to do with the Reformation, with the turn the Protestant ethic took in Prussia; in any event, it is a recurrent theme in the rosary of German idealism, from Kant to Fichte to Hegel, from Hegel to Marx. But I refuse to believe that we are dealing here with a specifically German obsession. After all, the utopian thinkers of Renaissance Italy, the theologians of Imperial Spain and the French Jacobins indulged quite heavily in the passion for consistency at any cost. And in our own century, dozens of nations, from Korea to Chile, from Cuba to Bulgaria, not to mention Nazi Germany and the Soviet Union, have organized their social systems on the basis of principles which are odiously threadbare and ludicrously hypocritical but which happen to be thoroughly consistent. (It is interesting to note that the models on which most existing one-party systems are constructed are of German origin.)

Entire continents are filled with the monotonous drone of unequivocal speech. In this type of rhetoric, decisions are always 'irrevocable', support is invariably 'staunch', the laws of history are 'iron', and determination is 'unflinching'. People who long for consistency are notoriously easy to organize in larger groups, in schools, churches, armies, sects or parties. The man who desperately wants to be 'true to himself' will end up, paradoxically, by surrendering to a collective identity. The private resolve to adhere to a set of principles and to follow them to their utmost consequences is no moral safeguard. Indeed there is often something schematic, something reminiscent of the bureaucrat, about an all too blatant devotion to principle. Those who pride themselves on their loyalty to ideas should remember that abstractions cannot be betrayed, only people.

Consistency, as a logical category, is empty. It is possible to be a consistent vegetarian, a consistent thief, Trotskyist, Mormon, dandy or Fascist. It is therefore not quite clear how consistency could ever lay claim to the status of a moral postulate. Another little problem arises as soon as one asks oneself whether consistency is to be understood as a demand on thoughts or on actions, or on both. In the first case, the risk to the outside world is minimal, but one may well end up a crank. Schelling's theory of electricity, for example, is entirely based on deduction. It is derived, with a great deal of precision, from the first principles of his *Naturphilosophie*, and is thus quite unblemished by empirical observation. With all due respect to a great mind, it must be said that it is complete nonsense, albeit of an entirely harmless and even entertaining kind. The point here is that consistency places an enormous strain on learning, and makes it exceedingly difficult for a change of mind to take place. If the postulate is then extended to include actions, some real trouble may be the result. The idea of Schelling fixing a light bulb according to his theories is almost too much to bear. And yet this is a relatively innocuous example. Quite a few brave and decent people, a decade or so ago, concluded from principles which I cannot call unsound that the best way to deal with napalm was to bomb Dow Chemical. Most of them have learned by experience to think otherwise, even at the cost of consistency. Those who refused to pay this price would seem to be in for a lifetime of attacking Dow Chemical with homemade explosives.

But even if one just happens to mind the slashing of welfare or of food-aid programmes to desperately poor countries, one ought to think twice before claiming consistency. Any such claim will lead to a particularly obnoxious sort of blackmail which has become very popular in certain quarters. As soon as one voices objections, some horribly well-groomed politician is sure to get up and say: This is all very well, but it is just talk. If you are so keen on foreign aid, or on the welfare of the poor, why not do something about it? Why not live up to your principles? Be consistent! If you happen to be a Christian, for example, the least one may ask for is that you go and spend the rest of your life in an African leper colony instead of sitting here and getting on our nerves. And if you don't like capitalism, why not go away and fight like Che Guevara?

This type of argument is not an argument at all; it is an echo of the voice which can be heard on the streets whenever a potential suicide is crouching high on the window-sill of an office building. It is the mob shouting: What are you waiting for? Why don't you jump? In Germany there was once a most courteous gentleman by the name of Adorno who had an answer to this cry. He said: 'The ability to distinguish between theory and practice is a great achievement of civilization.'

Now, given the confusing state of affairs which I have been describing, I should like to point out some of the advantages and even joys of inconsistency. I do not claim that inconsistency, in itself, is a virtue. There is something neutral and rather unassuming about it, and I dare say that it can be abused. I am not advocating incoherent babble, and I rather like rational discourse. Besides, the case for inconsistency cannot be made consistently without inviting a logical conundrum.

Instead, I would suggest that we owe our lives to vacillation, indecision and unprincipled action. You would not now be in a position to mind what I am saying, or agree with it, if it were not for the late Mr Khrushchev, who behaved, as we all know, like a disgraceful opportunist in 1962. Did he not back out with his rockets? Wasn't he simply yellow, as they say? Did he not throw overboard the most sacrosanct principles of Marxism–Leninism? And no one in the whole Kremlin had the guts to stand up and say selling out to imperialism is bad. No, all those old militants just had one thing on their minds; they wanted to save their own skins, and in the process they happened to save our skins as well. Consistency would have dictated quite a different course of action. It generally does. Let me mention just a few examples:

Take any economic doctrine whatsoever, apply it, proceed logically with your project, and you will eventually destroy the very economy you had set out to save.

Act out the fundamental tenets of capitalism to their ultimate consequences, and you will end up with a state of civil war and/or a Fascist dictatorship.

Attack the social system you live in by any means at your disposal, and you have terrorism; defend it by any means, and you have the Gestapo running the place.

Be a rigorous ecologist and defend nature against man with no holds barred, and you will end up leading a Stone Age existence.

Build communism, be uncompromising about it, and your

militancy will take you straight into what is rightly known as the socialist camp.

Pursue economic growth at any price and you will destroy the biosphere.

Join the armaments race, be consistent about it, and you will blow yourself to pieces.

Etcetera.

In this sort of situation, which has become quite frequent, principle isn't what it used to be. For those who are still looking around for a maxim to follow, I would suggest this: Consistency will turn any good cause into a bad one. It is a luxury which we can no longer afford. For philosophers who are interested in keeping their thinking as straight as possible, this must be an unwelcome thought, but for people at large it will not come as a surprise. In our parts of the world, a vast if not vociferous majority of citizens has come to realize, I believe, that their only chance of survival is based not on one or two Big Ideas, but on a constantly changing set of marginal options. They are quite prepared to face a lengthy and contradictory process of muddling through, of trial and error. Even in Germany, a society traditionally much given to principles, the last decades have seen a deep change in attitude. Social scientists have taken little note of this process, perhaps because they prefer to deal in Big Ideas or in statistical data. Nations as diverse as the Greeks and the Japanese, the Swedes and the Venezuelans, indeed most of the peoples who are given a chance to choose, will opt for the blessings of a more or less social democracy – not, I think, because of any deep-seated ideological conviction or loyalty, but because they feel instinctively that a sort of half-way house has become their only alternative to barbarism and self-destruction.

And now a word about ourselves. I hope you do not mind my using the first person of the plural form. Let us avoid categories such as 'the intelligentsia', or, even worse, 'the cultural workers', and just think of ourselves as a set of people who make a living by coming up, every now and then, with a new idea, a new image or a new shape. It is easy to see why the end of consistency is not something which we would relish. The state of affairs which I have tried to sketch goes against the grain of our most cherished habits. One of our main satisfactions in life has always been our ability to carry our ideas to extremes. Ever since we have existed as a social group – that is, for at least two centuries – we have been gainfully employed in going too far. Historically, the winner among us has always been the fellow who went further than anybody else. Never has this game of ours been played with greater fervour than in the first half of the twentieth century. In the heroic age of modernism, the logic of consistency was extremely powerful; the whole prestige of the avant-garde depends on its single-minded courage, on its determination to follow an ideological or aesthetic theorem to its very end.

It is true that not much blood was shed in the process. The radicalism of the Euro-American avant-garde did not lead to massacres. At worst it led to a certain amount of intolerance, sterility and dreariness. Thus we can afford to look back without anger to those days. There is even something touching about those black squares on the walls of museums and galleries, and about the critics who saw in them the culmination of art history. Some of us still remember the times when poets who filled a whole book with lower-case 'i's and 'e's were considered the salt of the earth. Treatises were written on the 'objective state of composition' as applied to the man who gave a one-hour talk 'On Nothing' in front of breathless audiences.

All these games, however, were innocent only as long as they were practised as an indoor sport. When architects started to write manifestos demanding that our cities be scrapped, this gave rise to shrill debates which must have been great fun. When they turned out to be consistent enough to reduce our living space to piles of white cubes, this had rather dire consequences, especially for the unfortunate people who were doomed to live and work in the ensuing concrete dreams. And wherever advanced political theories were consistently applied, things took a decidedly tragic turn.

9

In the late 1950s, the Political Science department of the University of Paris had become a very cosmopolitan place. All sorts of things were being taught: the political economy of under-developed nations; the importance of central planning; the modernization of traditional tribal societies; the dynamics of anti-colonialist revolutions ... It is therefore not surprising that the lectures and seminars of the faculty were largely frequented by a motley crowd of students from the former French colonial empire, from Vietnam and Morocco, from Madagascar and Somalia, from Algeria and Guyana.

Some of the more radical teachers had come to the conclusion that liberation movements in the poorest parts of the world would have to undo the structure of the colonial societies inherited from the age of imperialism, if they wanted to put an end to the endemic misery of their countries. It was no good, they said, to do away with foreign domination and to take power if existing social structures were left untouched. The radical solution which they advocated had three major aspects.

First of all, the relationship between town and country had to be reversed. The urbanization of the poor countries introduced by the colonial powers was disastrous. The parasitic cities siphoned off the productivity of the land. Industrialization would require a huge amount of foreign capital, and it would inevitably favour the local bourgeoisie. It should therefore be postponed. Absolute priority should be given to agriculture.

Second, a poor country must take care not to be integrated into the world market. Terms of trade would inevitably follow the pattern of international capitalism and perpetuate its domination. Isolation for a considerable length of time was the only solution. Economic self-sufficiency must be the goal. A subsistence economy would bring initial hardship for the more privileged part of the population, but it would permit autarky and thus, in the long run, put an end to exploitation from abroad.

Lastly, it was necessary to protect the underdeveloped countries from the baneful cultural influence of the West. It was held that the educated elites in post-colonial nations posed a threat to independence because they clung to the ideas and values of the metropolis. Merchants and functionaries, teachers and doctors were especially dangerous elements, since they had adopted Western ways in their formative years and would infest the whole nation with their thoughts and their lifestyles. This corrupting influence would have to be ended, and the bourgeoisie would have to be liquidated as a social class.

This programme, which was advocated by teachers from North Africa and Asia, and which was influenced by the Algerian war and by Maoism, is remarkable for a number of reasons. One of its more baffling aspects is the fact that it is curiously self-referential. Quite clearly, its proponents belonged to the educated elite in their own countries; they had spent their formative years in European schools, and their ideas are in great part derived from Western traditions. It would thus seem that they were, in terms of their own theory, at least as much part of the problem as they may have been part of any future solution. Granted that their ideas were based on the experiences of several poor countries, the empirical data they could draw upon still did not make any sense unless it was interpreted. And for this interpretation they depended on principles which they took over from European thought. Being progressive people, they did not avail themselves of the obscure dogmas and the ideological patent medicines which the West has produced in great abundance; they did not pick up political messages such as racism, chauvinism and anti-Semitism, which are very much part of our heritage. No, they took the very best we had to offer: the basic tenets of the French Revolution, the teachings of the Enlightenment, the idea that it was both necessary and possible to abolish the extremes of injustice, oppression and exploitation.

Among the students attending those courses were quite a few who came from South East Asia. One of them was called Kieu Samphan, another Jeng Sary, and a third one Saloth Sar, better known by his *nom de guerre* of Pol Pot. They all graduated with honours, packed up their notebooks, and went home. Fifteen years later they started to put into practice what their professors had taught them. They were very earnest, very devoted; their consistency cannot be doubted. The results are known to every-

*11*

body who reads newspapers or who owns a television set, and the only open question by now is whether the Khmer Rouge's experiment has claimed half a million or two and a half million lives. I try in vain to imagine what their teachers feel when they happen to think of their former pupils.

Mind you, I am not saying that it is a crime to follow a line of thought, *any* line of thought, to its ultimate logical conclusion. We are all extremely curious people who cannot bear to leave unthought anything that is thinkable, and we dearly wish to know where our latest hypothesis might take us. That, after all, is part of our work. Neither is there anything shameful about the fact that most of our trains of thought will sooner or later take us to a dead end. In a finite world, this is only to be expected. And if some of us feel like spending a lifetime in our respective blind alleys, this may seem a boring exercise, but, as long as it remains purely a matter of theory, I do not see why we should object to it. The little parable which I have just told goes to show, however, that some people are unable or unwilling to draw a line between theory and practice. They are so desperately consistent that they don't know a dead end when they see one. The fact that there is no way ahead inspires them to an ever more frenzied activity. The result, as we have seen, may well be murderous.

It must be said that there is a much simpler and less violent way out of a blind alley. Once you are sure that you have reached the end, and with a bit of foresight you can find out well in advance, you can turn around and try another route. The trouble is that people who have been nurtured on principles often feel that such a course of action spells defeat or even betrayal. Many of them have reached positions of great power. I am thinking of Mr Castro, Mr Begin, Mrs Thatcher and Mr Khomeini, to name just a few. In their respective dead ends, they hang on to their anachronistic dreams – terrifying remnants of these heroic days when a person could still imagine himself to have been in the right, just because history was on his side, and because the baddies were against him. In other words, by being sufficiently principled, and militant, and brave, a person could become, as it were, infallible.

Some of us may deplore the passing of the Age of Consistency. They might find some consolation in military science. The classic teachers of strategy have always held that there is no greater feat in warfare than orderly retreat from an untenable position. Only a fool bent on self-destruction will call such a move an act of cowardice. I would rather go along with Paul Feyerabend when he says: 'Stamping out opportunism will not make us better men; it will just make us more stupid. What we ought to get rid of is rather our tendency to dream up, in our egotistical way, some sort of "good" or "rational" or "responsible" life, which we then try to force down other people's throats in the guise of objective values.'

Inconsistency is not the answer to our predicament, but it has its advantages and its attractions. It cannot be preached. It increases our freedom of thought and our freedom of movement. It is good for our imagination. It is fraught with intellectual risks. It also takes a lot of training, but, if you put your mind to it, you may end up not only being less afraid, but even less afraid of being afraid. Inconsistency might even provide a much needed dose of irony and a measure of gaiety in the face of the prevailing mood of depression. We can never know what we have at the back of our minds, but most likely it is more than our principles allow for, and more than consistency will tolerate. Alas, the end of ideology is not in sight, and its monotonous noise seems to go on for ever. Amidst all the static and the clutter, the anachronism and the propaganda, nothing could be more tempting, and, perhaps more helpful, than the forbidden fruit of our brains.

Let me now jump to my conclusion, which may turn out to be quite different from yours. A tirade against consistency, however timely, may well bring comfort to the scatterbrained. Immersed as we are in the daily mush of the media, half-dazed by the relentless passage of trends and styles and quirks and fashions, exposed to the most banal and most routine sort of amnesia, an apology for the jellied mind is hardly what we need. To defend the charms of inconsistency is to ask for trouble. Misunderstanding being an essential mode of communication, some of you must have concluded that I have been making a plea on behalf of the Man without a Memory. I would therefore like to conclude with a tale in praise of obstinacy. Obstinacy, you see, is not a matter of principle. It does not need an ideological framework, and it does not offer justifications. The obstinate man is a modest animal, devoid of missionary ambition. He does not actually depend on a theory, and his deeds cannot be said to be derived from abstract postulates. His thoughts do not show up in opinion polls, and the technicians of political control will have a hard time making him out. He is also very difficult to organize. In short, he is a dangerous animal and, needless to say, there is no guarantee, there is only a possibility, that he will do some good. 'You go on talking as long as you like,' the obstinate man will say. 'I know what I want, and I'll keep my thoughts to myself.' Then, when he walks out of the door, he will drop a cryptic phrase. He will say: 'There is no other way.'

Take the inconspicuous man, for example, who is boarding the express train from Munich to Constance – for, although we can do without idols, we still need examples. Just look at him sitting across the aisle, in the smokers' compartment, a quiet, friendly fellow looking out at the dim November afternoon. It gets dark early at this time of year. He has grey eyes, he is in his mid-thirties, his clothes are old but neat, he looks like a craftsman, you can tell by his deft and slender hands. A mechanic probably, or a joiner. In his spare time he will go to his club and play the guitar or the accordion, and if he has some money left he will spend an evening at the small-town dance hall by the river. No, he does not read newspapers. Every now and then he will go to church on a rainy Sunday, but he does not really care deeply about religion, neither is he very much interested in politics.

Finally the train arrives in Constance. He gets off and walks alongside the lake. He obviously knows his way, but he does not seem to be in a hurry. There's an old suburb with overgrown gardens and warehouses. It is now a quarter to nine. In a minute or two, he will have reached the Swiss border. Two officers from the nearby customs post walk up and ask him for his papers. He produces his passport. It turns out that the document has expired a few weeks before, and so they ask him to empty his pockets. No contraband is found, but there are a few shreds of paper in his pocket, an old badge issued by the Red Front Militia ('It is just a memento,' he will explain later); some bolts and screws and springs, and finally there is a picture postcard showing the interior of a Munich beer cellar called the Bürgerbräu. The customs men don't quite know what to do with him. In the end they ask him to come along for a routine check.

While he is sitting down on a bench in the office hut – the wall calendar shows the date 8 November 1939, and it is now exactly 9.10 p.m. – a bomb explodes in Munich, three minutes after Adolf Hitler has left, earlier than planned, the beer cellar where the big Nazi November rally has been held. Georg Elser had spent four months making the bomb before planting it in a pillar of the Bürgerbräu vaults.

Elser, born on 4 January 1903 in Hermaringen, and murdered in Dachau concentration camp on 9 April 1945, Hitler's most dangerous enemy, did not belong to any organized group, nor did he act on the orders of any party. In planning, preparing and carrying out his attempt to kill Hitler, he was entirely on his own. There is no trace of his story in the textbooks used in German schools. In the scholarly works of German historians, Elser figures in a footnote if he is mentioned at all.

Experts will tell you we are living in a society made up of manipulated zombies, and that there are now entire generations suffering from anomie, narcissism and loss of self. They may well have a point. But I think that obstinate man is still very much with us, just as he was forty or four hundred years ago. You will meet him at the next street corner if you look out for him. He has no specific sociological location. Obstinacy is not a privilege of the intellectuals, quite the contrary. I believe that it will never disappear, but I cannot offer any proof for this contention. I cannot explain where people like Elser come from, what makes them tick, or what may be the source of their determination. Like most of the things worth bearing in mind, it remains an open question.

*(1981)*

## 2

## Reluctant Eurocentrism:

## A Political Picture Puzzle

The intellectual world has its own deadly sins, which are not to be found in the catechism. As if they didn't have their hands full with envy and gluttony, pride and fascination, the intellectuals are constantly inventing (and trespassing against) new prohibitions. Venerable and familiar names, like those listed in the confessional – sloth, avarice, pride – are out of the question as sins for the intelligentsia; they lack the high-quality scientific cachet, the watermark of abstraction.

Nor can the deviations of consciousness put in a claim for consecration by eternity. A wrathful god who would separate the white from the black sheep is not in sight, and the world spirit has fallen silent too. Rather, it's the watchdogs of whatever doctrine is dominant, if not indeed of fashion, who take care that the villain is exposed and the upright man is rewarded. So whoever sins intellectually, by no means risks eternal damnation. At worst he is reviled for a while, pulled apart by critics or completely ignored. A few years or decades pass, a new register of sins is agreed upon, and the formerly depraved deviationist is rehabilitated. Anticommunism, for example, an aberration which was considered unforgivable among enlightened people for decades is today altogether socially acceptable again, indeed it is almost *de rigueur*.

It's quite a different matter, however, with the cardinal intellectual sin of the seventies, a mode of thought which bears the curious name Eurocentrism; its reprehensibility, I believe, remains unquestioned even today.

*17*

The Europeans noticed quite early on that they are not alone in this world; and they turned this circumstance to their advantage quite early on. The history of our 'discoveries' consisted, as we know, of colonizing the inhabitants of other continents, and that means conquering and robbing them.

Ethnology, a new science of humanity, owes its development to this bloody process. Its Anglo-Saxon representatives have introduced the ambitious name 'anthropology' for their subject, a variation which, for lack of specialist knowledge, I would rather leave unexamined. After the seafarers and the soldiers, the adventurers and the missionaries, the planters and the engineers, the travelling scholars also fanned out in their turn, to discover what kind of peoples were to be converted and robbed, civilized and exterminated, there in the remotest regions of the earth.

The more intelligent among the anthropologists soon noticed that their researches were leading them into an epistemological and moral labyrinth. Because it was precisely what interested them most, the otherness of what used to be called the primitive peoples, the savages, the barbarians, the coloured races, which remained inaccessible, and that not only because the latter received them with a mistrust that was all too justified.

But the real hindrance to research was the researcher himself, together with his discipline. It was this, like everything else that the ethnologist brought with him – his gaze, his standards, his prejudices, his language – which placed itself between him and what he wanted to investigate, and so he ran the risk of bringing home only dead facts and living errors. His arrival alone was already a considerable invasion of the societies he wanted to observe, an interference factor of incalculable magnitude.

It is not surprising therefore, that (as the ethnologist Fritz Kramer has shown in a brilliant book) the booty of anthropological research consists largely of European fancies. It's our own reflection that perpetually appears on the projection screen of science; only we have no desire to recognize ourselves in it.

Ways of escaping ethnology's dilemma are few and risky. Of course, it is possible to postulate the equality of all human societies and to raise the demand that every community must be described and judged on the basis of its own conditions. But that is easier said than done. A consistent relativism assumes an observer who would be in a position to leave his own cultural baggage at home. Such a scientist would not only have to be a master of brainwashing, he would also have to be capable of using it on himself. Only then would he, as an ethnologist, be completely free of his 'European' prejudices – but along with them of his science as well.

Another way of solving the dilemma – it could be called the existential one – is to gamble one's own identity. The researcher becomes a kind of renegade. He joins his Melanesians, Nahuas, Malagasies in the bush. *He goes native*: that's what in their day the English colonial rulers called the irregular, unscientific form of such a change of identity. In anthropology, a mild version of this method is described as 'participant observation'. The stranger adapts to the way of life he meets with, he tries to penetrate the mentality of the peoples with whom he is staying, by transforming himself into a Melanesian, Nahua, Malagasy.

It is evident that such experiments do not spirit away the original dilemma. They lead rather into an extensive maze of ambiguities. Because the researcher's transformation is an experiment with a time limit, an as-if, which once again divides him from his hosts. His ulterior motive remains intact. The anthropologist becomes an actor, a ventriloquist or a spy.

These are roles which a respectable academic finds difficult. Anthropology as a swings and roundabout of culture and identity: not all researchers would be prepared to come to terms with such a definition. A minority sought and found a way out of the dilemma in the politicization of their discipline. They took the side of the oppressed and threatened peoples who were the object of their work. Some of these radical renegades saw the civilization from which they came as the principal enemy of humanity. In accordance with the maxim 'the last shall be the first' they believed in the future of the 'savages' and demonstrated their solidarity with them. And it was they who coined the term Eurocentrism and turned it polemically against their academic colleagues who preferred to remain what they were:

professors in Uppsala and Göttingen, in Louvain, Cambridge and Paris.

All in all an esoteric business, one of those theoretical bones on which a small band of specialists gnaws in quiet and with some pleasure. So it might appear, and so indeed it was, until about twenty years ago. In the short period of time which has passed since then, the problem of Eurocentrism has irreversibly established itself in our consciousness – yes, one can say that in its most general and trivial form it has become a platitude.

The historical reasons are obvious. The collapse of European colonial rule in its traditional form, the liberation movements in Asia, Africa and Latin America and the political, economic and ideological consequences of this global process have fundamentally altered our picture of the world.

We have learned that we are in the minority, and that those others, the majority, are not hanging around somewhere on the periphery of the inhabited world as passive objects of our economic interests and our scientific curiosity. Such knowledge is not gained voluntarily; it only establishes itself when there is no other possibility.

Only thirty years ago Europeans and North Americans could still ignore the most enormous events without much effort; the Chinese Civil War, the colonial massacres in Indonesia and Madagascar were only hazily noticed. That only changed with the Algerian War, the Cuban revolution, the conflict in the Near East and the wars in Indochina. The brightly coloured scenes from the cigarette card album, the wax figures in the ethnological museum came to life, they turned up in person in the living room. The TV screen teemed with evidence. A problem that until then a couple of anthropologists had discussed in their tent or in a seminar, became the common property of primary school teachers and leader writers, of social workers and parish priests.

Really understanding what was now on the agenda of history was another matter. That is obvious even from the attempts to give the state of affairs a name. The crudest terms were good enough to indicate the breach which had opened up before our eyes: over here the developed, over there the underdeveloped countries, over here the poor, over there the rich countries; and the confrontation between them was sometimes called the international class struggle, and sometimes, in the euphemistic vocabulary of Social Democracy, the North–South conflict. In a futile effort to label an explosion, the majority of the others in Asia, Africa and Latin America were given the name 'the Third World'.

That this was not a concept, but a portmanteau, a semantic all-purpose term, became clear in the seventies at the latest, when the oil-producing countries became the moguls of the world economy while in Africa and Indochina whole countries more or less starved.

Has there ever been a European who seriously believed that the yellow races were yellow? Did you really think that the Savages were savage, the Coloureds coloured, the Primitives primitive? Did you perhaps think that the explosion of the world could be numbered one, two and three? What can China and Niugini have in common, for example? If they have a common denominator at all, then it can only be defined negatively – and that is from our perspective: as lack. These people were missing something, whether it was history or development, a god or a state. And with that we have arrived at Eurocentrism again.

Wolfgang B. from Nördlingen, for example, has had himself driven to the top of Victoria Peak even though it's late afternoon. He looks towards China over the glittering skyscrapers, the harbour and the bay and he has to admit the panorama is unique. He's a model-builder by profession, one of the best model-builders in the world probably, *en route* to Guangzhou, formerly Canton. He's going to construct a complex industrial plant for the trade fair on a scale of 1:30, a toy which doesn't reveal at first glance that the cost is going to run into billions.

Wolfgang B. is an unprejudiced man, he has read books, Edgar Snow, a biography of Mao, a report from a Chinese village. He is looking forward to China, and as far as Hong Kong is concerned two days' holiday have been enough for him to notice some flaws in the weave of this paradise. He has never studied sociology; quotes from Engels don't flow from his lips on his walks through Kowloon. Instead, he has the habit – simply because of his job – of looking very carefully at what he sees; so, too, at the slums of Hong Kong, the fragile boats of the refugees, the overcrowded blocks of flats, the prostitution, the traffic chaos.

He notices that an omnipresent mafia controls the street-traders, the night life and the smuggling; that the sales-girls, the waiters, the employees in the travel agencies play the Stock Exchange, a kind of Chinese roulette with forward merchandise option deals and gold-mine shares; that the Hong Kong police is exceptionally corrupt; and that real-estate speculation has reached terroristic dimensions. Hong Kong is the most beautiful of capitalism's Asiatic dependencies. But the neat promenades, the extravagantly luxuriant parks, the faded dignity of the Hong Kong Club don't delude model-builder Wolfgang B. as to its wolflike character. Only he would express himself a little more succinctly; after all he isn't an assistant professor.

Fourteen days later, the job in the People's Republic has been concluded, the model completed and handed over to the prospective Chinese buyers, Wolfgang B. begins the return journey. He sits in the air-conditioned express train that links Guangzhou with Hong Kong and feels surprised. He's surprised that he's looking forward to Hong Kong, that he can hardly wait to step out of the train. He'll take a quite ordinary taxi, not the big limousine from the Ministry as in Guangzhou. No one will brief him, look after him, patronize him, supervise and instruct him. He will sleep alone in a room without official permission, or not sleep alone in a room, and eat and drink when and where and what he wants. He won't buy himself a diamond-studded watch, neither does he need a Rolls-Royce; but a newspaper in which news is to be found wouldn't be bad, a little naturalness wouldn't be bad. Wolfgang B. thinks of Guangzhou with its crumbling façades, its black-market traders, its sad old men. At the border he heaves a sigh. He can't slip out of his skin.

Eurocentrism – is that model-builder Wolfgang B.'s sin, or is he only suffering from homesickness, a longing which, as we well know, does not only draw on the good, true and beautiful things but attaches itself with particular stubbornness to the shabby, the questionable and the defective?

But why then does Wolfgang B., a native Swabian, feel at home in Hong Kong?

If it was only that! But I sat on the same train, and I was told that in the river which forms the border and which the train crosses, the floating bodies of the drowned are found again and again; others have themselves nailed up in containers in order to get over the border to Hong Kong, a dangerous method because it's possible to suffocate in the attempt. These unfortunates, too, are envoys of the overwhelming majority, just as much as those Chinese who legally, for whatever reason, travel from one world to another on the Guangzhou–Hong Kong express and stock up from the hostess with American soft drinks, French *petits fours* and English cigarettes.

It's the commodities that tell the truth; the cassette recorders in the souks of Damascus, the Seiko watches in the shop windows of Peking, the jeans and the sunglasses, the whiskies, the perfumes and the cars. Above all the cars. No victorious liberation front, no starving tropical country, no pedagogic dictatorship, no matter how puritanical, gets by without them. Electrically controlled sliding windows, air conditioning, tinted and bullet-proof glass, stereo, automatic locking devices – all inclusive.

This frenetic desire to imitate is a worldwide phenomenon whose implications no one has yet thought through to the end. Its effects are like those of a natural force, they are as irresistible and as little responsible to the control of reason as an avalanche. There has certainly been no shortage of attempts to analyse rationally the needs of poor and underdeveloped countries. Again and again intermediate technologies were proposed in order to relate the structures of traditional societies to the demands of industrialization.

After years of work, the engineers of a European car company developed a vehicle adapted to the conditions of poor tropical countries. Built on a simple modular principle, it didn't need any care, was economical, easy to repair and handle; it was also cheap, since all unnecessary accessories were missing. This car never went into production, since the countries concerned firmly refused to drive cheaper cars than the French or the Americans.

This confidence, or rather this lack of confidence, is not only to be observed in the drawing-board states of Central Africa; even great nations with a great past are not free from it. In China a luxury limousine is still being manufactured today which matches in every detail a Russian vehicle from the fifties, which in its turn is copied from a forties American Packard. This copy of a copy moreover bears the name 'Red Flag'.

On its sky-blue cover the Shanghai telephone directory shows happy people gazing at a sky which is pierced by television towers, rockets and satellites. The text is interspersed with black and white adverts and coloured plates in which European-looking models display European women's fashions. The pieces of furniture are exact copies of those splay-legged side-tables, dressing tables and wardrobes which we remember from the Adenauer era. The whole book is a slim version of the Necker-mann mail-order catalogue of 1957.

Now I haven't the least wish to poke fun at this evidence of Chinese modernization policy. It's much too depressing for that. What makes one's heart sink is not the fact that the population of a poor country is insisting gently but with elementary force on an improvement in its living standards, but the path of compulsive imitation that it adopts in doing so. It seems as if every mistake, every whim, every folly of the West has to be repeated, as if no deformation, no wrong turning can be left out.

Every chair, every bottle of lemonade, is a slavish imitation of a foreign model, as if it would be unthinkable to invent something of one's own, even if only a new reading-lamp or radio cabinet. It's inevitable that the copy is inferior to the original. It's not only the shortage of materials, and the industrial shortcomings that ensure that this is so; rather it's in the nature of the process itself, that the out of date, the stale and the shabby triumphs whenever a society puts up with living at second hand.

But, you will object, a society doesn't consist of commodities. Let the Chinese and the Peruvians, the Congolese and the Pakistanis make themselves comfortable however they like; the main thing is that they manage to get hold of the most essential things of all that a human being needs in order to live, a pair of shoes, a bowl of food, a doctor who can bind their wounds. No one can dispute that. But the commodities propagate something beyond their immediate consumption. At just that point at which each person has his shoes, his bowl, his surgeon – and this goal has been achieved in China – they prophesy the future victory of a single culture. But this culture is not Chinese.

Or do you think it doesn't make any difference whether someone carries out calculations with an abacus or with a computer? What happened to *us* at that moment when we sat down behind a steering wheel for the first time, alone, in our own car? Our tools, machines and products have altered us beyond recognition. Our idiotic architecture, our supermarkets, our three-room apartments, our cosmetics, our television programmes which are spreading across the whole world are only individual elements of an evidently irresistible totality.

We've experienced more than one fiasco with 'the iron laws of history', but a person who watches television is very different from someone who listens to stories. A Marxist thesis, which no one has yet refuted, says that the unfettered productive forces of capitalist industry make short shrift of every recalcitrant legacy, every autonomous 'superstructure'. They are the bulldozer of world history, which clears away everything which blocks its way and levels every traditional culture.

And the commodities, appliances and machines are only the most visible part of what the 'developing countries' import. We supply them with weapons and toxins, techniques of government and propaganda. Even the symbols of their sovereignty are slavish imitations of what they believe they have liberated themselves from through bloody struggles; the idea of the nation, the slogans of the revolution, the concept of the party, the emblems of statehood from national anthem to constitution, from flag to protocol.

Khomeini owes his victory to the cassettes of the Philips company, Amin commanded his gang of murderers in finery that was nothing more than a grotesque imitation of a British general's uniform. Ghaddafi equipped his killers with the technical know-how of the West German Federal CID and Soviet advisers call the tune in the corridors of the interior ministries of Cuba and Mozambique. Among the 'West's' inventions which are eagerly copied throughout the world are not only aftershave and the deep-freeze, but also the electric shock and the concentration camp. The *idée fixe* of progress is increasingly being questioned by Europeans and North Americans; it dominates unchallenged only in the 'developing countries' of Asia, Africa and Latin America. The true Eurocentrics are the others.

It is probably fair to say that there is a lot of cant in Western anti-imperialist discourse. There is, by now, a long tradition of self-criticism in our part of the world, particularly on the Left. Ever since the beginning of the twentieth century, it has been commonplace to complain about the decadence of Western civilization, a thesis which has strong roots in conservative thought. Marxist theory has emphasised the economic exploitation of colonial and ex-colonial societies, but simplistic preachers have long since reduced serious analysis to a sort of zero–sum game, arguing that industrial societies live by pilfering the Third World: '*We* are rich because *they* are poor.' In the course of time the myth of the Noble Savage has been resurrected in the shape of *tiers-mondisme*. The polemic against 'consumerism' has been a mainstay of the opposition ever since the sixties. Inevitably, idealist notions engender a rhetoric rich in banality and bad faith. An opposition based on them may be subjectively well meant, but sooner or later it is bound to founder, because there is no mediation between its 'convictions' and the social reality which it seeks to transform. The result is, even from a strictly moral point of view, painfully ambiguous: the Left is just as Eurocentric as the rest of us. Its only distinction is a bad conscience, reluctant Eurocentrism.

Others, however, and perhaps they are the best among us, take a different decision. I'm not thinking about the drilling engineers in their air-conditioned ghettos, or the businessmen in their private jets, or the mercenaries, policemen and marines, but about the doctors on the Cambodian border and the agronomists in the Sahel; about people who have given up their three-room apartments in Wuppertal or St Louis in order to train mechanics somewhere in the bush or sink wells in the desert.

The readiness to render spontaneous, altruistic aid appears so strange under prevailing conditions that one responds with perplexity to such nonconformists. Some admire them, others call them, with a certain dubious respect, idealists. Yet others shake their heads or even believe them to be unsuspecting tools of some imperialist plot.

That is always unjust and usually wrong. Nevertheless, it is still necessary to enquire about the inner motives and the meaning of that solidarity with the 'Third World' that stirs here and there in the industrial countries of the West. Official development aid doesn't need to concern us any further; its political and economic goals are not secret after all. It is a matter of spheres of influence, raw materials, export interests. The development policies of every industrial power East or West are the continuation of colonial policies by other means.

Anyone, on the other hand, who risks his life as a doctor in order to dress the wounds of rebels or refugees in some African civil war has something else in mind; and something of this larger interest is also to be found among those who have stayed at home, working on obscure committees to raise money for imprisoned trade unionists in Bolivia. The self-deceptions to which such a commitment can lead are well-known, and it's also no secret that the ritual playing of Chilean protest songs in Berlin bars had no noticeable influence on the bloody course of events in that country.

But independently of that, of how seriously or half-heartedly, of how effectively or how ineffectively the helpers of the 'Third World' may go to work, they are agreed on one point, and this point is the decisive one: they all identify themselves with a cause which is not their own. In this respect they are the successors of those ethnologists who understood themselves as cultural renegades. The Dane who makes the problems of the Eskimos his own, the student from Massachusetts who organizes a lobby for the defence of the Brazilian Indians: all these people want to help not only others but themselves too, and that is completely legitimate.

One could perhaps call what they are looking for among those distant peoples the utopian minimum. The stubborn hope which they place in the future of the 'Third World' corresponds to their scathing critique of the society which produced them and which has consumed any utopian surplus. The ideological shreds of Marxism or religion in which some of them clothe their search cannot conceal the fact that the goal of this search is to find the 'completely other'.

But what if this 'completely other' doesn't exist? These peoples, proud of their own traditions, unhampered by 'consumerism', less decadent and ruined, but older, purer, less corruptible than we are, pursuing their own project despite sacrifices and hardships – perhaps they only exist in the imagination of those who are looking for them?

And does this search not also have a disagreeable side? Does it not reproduce the old dilemma of the anthropologist, forever confronted by his own ghosts in the stranger's mirror. Is the 'Third World' in the end nothing more than a projection?

At any rate there's something odd about the enthusiasm with which many visitors from the industrialized world regard the Spartan features of some 'liberation movements'. Someone who, having flown 4000 miles, enthuses about the unique dignity of the rice farmers cultivating their fields with their bare hands standing knee deep in the mud, deserves to have his behaviour called moral cretinism rather than solidarity. And what about the iron social control, the sexual repression, the dull-witted formalism, the bureaucratic despotism which weighs upon large parts of the underdeveloped world? We can't judge that from our position, these are transitional phenomena, the people there have different needs ... Admittedly that wouldn't be right for us, but in their circumstances ... And so on.

Is that not the most naked racism masked as sympathy? Is it asking too much for an American in Angola, a Swede in China, a German in Cuba, to say to himself, at least once a day, as an experiment: These people are just like us? And that means that they do not only want schools and hospitals, canteens and barracks. They want to choose their profession just like us. They want to love one another. They want to have the choice. They want to have freedom of movement. They want to think for themselves and make decisions for themselves. And apart from that they want machines instead of flails, cars instead of hand-carts, refrigerators, holiday trips, telephones, three-room apartments. Just like us.

Poor Pasolini resisted this truth to the point of self-destruction. His utopia of the 'Third World' didn't flinch from any conclusion. It didn't just put up with poverty; it elevated it into a virtue. To this moralist underdevelopment appeared as paradise lost; a paradise which was cruel and hard but also humane. He found this 'Third World' in his own country, in the backward regions of Italy and he watched as it was gradually destroyed by industrial progress. Disappointment over this loss put Pasolini in a rage which was as clear-headed as it was reckless. In the end he reviled the very people he wanted to protect from this crime: his countrymen who were fleeing the chronic underdevelopment of the South, to look for a better life. And for them that meant looking for the world which promised them cars, television and three-room apartments and which in the eyes of Pasolini, who was murdered in his own sports car, was corrupt and the devil's work.

Since the abandonment of the last alternative project of history, that of Mao Zedong, only one future seems still to be left. The peoples of Asia, Africa and Latin America have fallen under the spell of a universal cargo cult: everything new, whether for good or ill, comes from the industrial countries, and everything old must be sacrificed to the new.

But the massive approval which our civilization receives does not fill us with triumph. On the contrary, it disappoints us, irritates us, makes us uneasy. We have no desire to be number one. We long ago got out of the habit of regarding Europe as the navel of the world, and we find the idea that the future of the human race could resemble a migration of lemmings led by us altogether depressing.

There are several reasons, subjective and objective, good and bad, why we don't like to be confronted by the Eurocentrism of the underdeveloped. It is not an uplifting thought to be flagbearers of a civilization whose catastrophic potential becomes more obvious year by year. It has never been the case before in history that humanity has staked everything on a single card. To a certain extent it lived scattered in a great number of autonomous cultures, each one pursuing its own project. Looked at in that way, the Tower of Babel had its positive side: far from coming to terms with one another, a multiplicity of societies evolved, inventing specific solutions for their own survival. With the industrial revolution this diversity began to disappear. Its last remnants are being liquidated before our eyes. That's not only sad, it's very dangerous; because the more homogeneous a population is, the more susceptible it is to catastrophes and the gloomier are its prospects for the future.

Besides, it's as good as certain that our able successors in the poorer countries are backing the wrong horse. A simple computer projection of their needs and of the resources which would be required to generalize the material standards of the Western industrial countries demonstrates the hopelessness of such an undertaking. Three billion cars, 400 million tons of meat, 40 million gigawatt hours of electricity, 12 billion tons of oil per annum. The planet which is our home can't provide all that. The consequences of unchanged targets are wars of distribution, extortion, vast conflicts. The 'Third World's' enthusiastic willingness to learn does not only worry us for noble reasons. The closer industrial progress gets to the ecological limits of capacity, the more our civilization resembles a zero–sum game: one player's gain is another's loss.

But the existence of the others with projects that weren't ours, the existence of fundamentally different cultures somewhere out there in the jungle, in the taiga, in the desert, was also a psychological comfort to the 'civilized' of the earth. These distant neighbours meant a relief from the strain. They allowed us to dream of another, lost life. Whenever the price we had to pay for progress was hurting us, we thought of the others, savages, blacks, bedouins, orientals, nomads, Eskimos, hunters, Malays, inhabitants of mythical islands; the naive patchwork of a colourful humanity, that was different from us, and with whom our disappointed hopes found an ambiguous refuge. We imposed upon the others what our own industrialized existence denied us, desires, promised lands, utopias. This method of projection is deeply rooted in the European tradition. I even believe that the internationalism of the Left in Europe and North America derives for the greatest part from such sources. So the revolutionary hope which has come to nothing is transferred further and further into the distance, first to Russia and Central Asia, then to China and to the so-called Third World.

It is time to take leave of such dreams. It was always an illusion that liberation could be delegated to the faraway others; today this self-deception has become a threadbare evasion. An exotic alternative to industrial civilization no longer exists. We are encircled and besieged by our own imitations.

Their worries are different from ours. How does a poor country achieve primary accumulation? How can an unstable nation be consolidated? How can steel production be increased? How can agriculture be mechanized? These are questions which were on the agenda in Europe and North America a hundred years ago. It is part of the fateful inheritance of the underdeveloped countries that they are unable to set themselves any historically new problems. That is a consequence of their situation and not, as the incorrigible racists among us imagine, of some kind of original inferiority. (A parenthesis for idiots of this kind, who, it is to be feared, will never die out: take a look at the Chinese physicists in Princeton, the Indian biochemists in Berkeley, the Iranian surgeons in Holland. And who built glittering Hong

Kong? The 2 per cent who are white, and live there more tolerated than determining, or the 98 per cent who are Chinese? It is
all simply and solely a question of social context. So much for the
obvious. Close parenthesis.)

It is the West that remains, spreading out in every direction.
The new problems are being posed here, and here alone, and
here alone are to be found, sparingly enough, the new solutions.
Not too much has occurred to us in recent decades: apart from
birth control, ecology, feminism, they have been, above all, technological tricks – microcomputers, means of communication,
and decisive steps in basic research, principally in molecular
biology.

But perhaps, behind our backs as it were, something else has
happened that would be much more momentous. Perhaps that
savage, distant, brightly coloured diversity which was external to
our civilization has immigrated into its centres. The increasing
dangerousness of everyday life in the great cities of the West
would be one indication of that. The more the exotic is eliminated worldwide and the more traditional diversity is made to
conform, the more the industrial societies become a patchwork
internally. Not only the United States, but also France, Sweden,
West Germany are melting pots today, multiracial states. Ethnic
minorities, subcultures, political and religious sects establish
themselves in the metropoles. This unpredictable confusion is
not only a result of immigration from outside, its roots lie in the
same historic continent that gave birth to industrial growth.

The vitality of the West derives, in the end, from the negativity
of European thinking, its eternal dissatisfaction, its voracious
unrest, its *lack*. Doubt, self-criticism, self-hate, even, are its most
important productive forces. It's our strength that we can't
accept ourselves and what we have produced. That's why we
regard Eurocentrism as a sin of consciousness. Western civilization lives from whatever calls it into question, whether it's
barbarians or anarchists, Red Indians or Bolsheviks. And if a
cultural other is no longer available, then we just produce our
own savages; technological freaks, political freaks, psychic freaks,
cultural freaks, moral freaks, religious freaks. Confusion, unrest,

ungovernability are our only chance. Disunity makes us strong.

From now on we have to rely on our own resources. No Tahiti is in sight, no Sierra Maestre, no Sioux and no Long March. Should there be such a thing as a saving idea, then we'll have to discover it for ourselves.

*(1980)*

# 3

## The Highest Stage of Underdevelopment: A Hypothesis about Really Existing Socialism

### TRUE STORIES

1. *The One-eyed.* Set an hour aside on the day before your departure. Choose a medium-sized suitcase and go to a department store. Buy everything by the dozen: lipsticks, pocket calculators, tights, typewriter ribbons, electric razors. The things you bring must be small and light. Remember the customs! In the place you're travelling to, foreign trade is a state monopoly. Commodities from the West are out of reach to anyone who does not belong to the wafer-thin layer of the privileged; on the black market one has to lay out a worker's weekly wage for such insignificant objects. In these circumstances the contents of your suitcase assume a virtually magical value. Because you know all about that, you've also remembered the sunglasses. The sales assistant in Frankfurt was somewhat surprised you took a whole dozen at once. She immediately removed the gold labels with the trade name from the tinted glass. A serious error! For once at your destination you discover that it's these very plastic butterflies that constitute the fetish value of the glasses. They guarantee the foreign origin of the goods and must under no circumstances be removed. The *jeunesse dorée* of the country wear their blue, brown, green tinted or mirrored sunglasses even in the rain; even in a darkened room; even at night. Only the right side is of any use, the owner is blind on his left side; he sees only

the back of the label. The wearers of these glasses are called, half enviously, half ironically, 'the one-eyed'.

2. *The State Visit.* The motorway from the airport to the centre of the capital is hermetically sealed off; flags, banners, flag-waving schoolchildren everywhere. In the afternoon the state guest is shown the latest triumph of the plan; a truck assembly plant. The minister guides the delegation through the halls, the workforce lines the route. All the engineers are local! All achieved by our own efforts! However, to celebrate the occasion the machinery is silent.

Not until two hours after the armour-plated Mercedes has left do soldiers of the security forces, armed with sub-machine-guns, open two inconspicuous steel doors and allow the two hundred and fifty or so foreign managers, engineers and skilled workers who have built up the plant and kept it going, to leave the boiler room in which they have been locked up for the duration of the inspection. It's difficult to say who was supposed to be deceived by this trick; after all, the whole city knew that the assembly plant had been constructed by an Italian company, and anyone who wanted to know all the details only needed to turn to the *Financial Times.*

3. *The Plug.* The American couple from Atlanta, whom you got to know in the lift (there is only a single lift for the almost two hundred rooms of the hotel, the other has been out of order for months) are outraged. The couple had booked a trip to this country because 'they've already been everywhere' – an adventurous decision which they now regret. It's already sufficient provocation for an estate agent from Georgia to have to fall back on the services of a state travel agency: in this country tourism is, of course, a state monopoly. You feel sorry for the man. You carefully explain to him that you can't understand why he's upset. All right, he pays 120 dollars a night, and it's true that the air-conditioning makes an infernal racket but only produces a weak,

stale breath of air. But on the other hand he's got a whole suite! Next to the bedroom there's an ante-chamber which is as large as a medium-sized gym and which contains two out-of-tune pianos. Perhaps it's the patches of rust on the eternally dripping bathtubs that irritate him? If only that was all! No, the bathtub doesn't have a plug. Having reached this point in the conversation you laughingly draw a black object out of your trouser pocket.

'You didn't know that?' you ask insincerely. Everyone who knows his way around here, travels with his own rubber plug. Plugs are worth more than their weight in gold; because although this country does have a bathtub factory of its own, they've forgotten about the plugs. After all, Bob, the authorities couldn't remember everything! The plug is, as it were, the lowest common denominator of all infrastructural problems. You may perhaps have to do without your bath, but in return you have been given a profound insight into this society's economic life!

4. *The Cheese.* Imagine that you are here as a guest of the government. One evening someone knocks at the door of your room. You open it, and two armed men in uniform come in. One of them has, in his hand, a small package, which he gives to you. You sign a receipt, and the two soldiers leave the room saluting. A printed card with personal greetings from the dictator hangs from the string of the package. You unwrap the present. To your astonishment it is a Camembert.

So next you pick up the telephone and make some enquiries. This is what you find out. The dictator cherishes a passion for cattle-farming. He owns a private dairy farm. He had the cows flown in from Europe, as well as the milking machines and the centrifuges. Animal geneticists, dairy experts, veterinary surgeons from Switzerland are on hand to support the scheme in every way. Although cheese is not only unknown as a foodstuff in this part of the world, but also useless, the dictator takes the view that whatever the French can do, he can do too. The animals, however, are not equal to the tropical climate; the costs (in Western currency) are prohibitive, each Camembert costs as much as a small tractor.

The next morning you discover that news of the favour you have been granted has spread right round the capital. You are congratulated. The negotiations with the authorities make rapid progress, all the problems have disappeared, you are envied by everyone. The Camembert tastes distinctly of ammonium chloride and at 38°C in the shade is completely inedible.

5. *The Booth.* You simply can't avoid a visit to the steelworks. You can count yourself lucky that it's not the local party committee who's showing you round, but your interpreter, a cheerful fellow who always has his guitar with him, tells risqué jokes, and in the evening when he has to write his informer's reports, asks you for ideas and suggestions. You notice a little wooden booth in the main factory hall. In it sits an elderly man lost in thought, head resting on his hands. After the conducted tour comes lunch in the canteen, and the customary toasts. On the way back, you pass the booth again. The man is still sitting there, idle, his mind elsewhere, a pile of peanut shells on the table in front of him. No one bothers about him. You ask your interpreter what this odd fish is doing in the noisy and somewhat chaotic plant.

'Oh, that's engineer S., he has to be left in peace, he's got sorrows.'

It turns out that after his wife left him, S. became depressed. Asked when the misfortune has occurred his colleagues reply: 'We don't quite remember any more. Maybe it was three years ago, maybe it was five, and since then he just sits there. He has to be left in peace.'

6. *The Baby-bottle.* You've got a headache once again, no wonder in this climate. A good thing that the chemist is on

your way. Drugs are ridiculously cheap here, twenty Aspirin – which, by the way, aren't called Aspirin – cost less than a penny. Odd that there's such a crowd; but the chemist already knows you and beckons to you. You don't need to stand in a queue here. As you are about to pay for the pills, the assistant hisses in your ear, 'baby-bottles have come in'. You don't understand what he is trying to say. But the chemist pulls a half-wrapped bottle from under the counter and presses it into your hand. 'With rubber!' he whispers. At last you realize that this is a sensation, and you acquire one of the marvellous bottles for a derisory sum of money. Leaving the chemist's you discover that in the meantime a queue a hundred yards long has formed outside the shop. Unwittingly, you have acquired an object for which at any time, through barter, you can obtain lightbulbs, writing paper, toothpaste, perhaps even a canister of petrol.

7. *The Puddle.* These ugly, six-storey apartment blocks at the edge of the city, completed four years ago, could also be on the outskirts of Barcelona, Osaka or Milan. However, no speculators were at work here, only the state. Apart from the cracked balconies and the damp patches on the façade, the building looks depressing and shabby, but not uninhabitable. But the entrance is like a building site. Where the pathway should be, there's a shallow pit. The residents have laid a couple of planks across the muddy pool. Housewives and children balance carefully across this improvised footbridge. Every time the spring thaw comes, the water rises, excrement floating on it.

Foreigners are rarely seen out here. After years have passed someone who is perhaps especially naive, or especially obstinate, begins to ask questions. How long has it been like this here, he wants to know from his friends, who have a tiny flat on the third floor. Reply: It's always been like that. Who is to blame, who's responsible for it? Weary smile. Couldn't one complain? Shrugs. A petition signed by all the residents, a delegation sent to the appropriate administration office. Nervous attempts to change the subject. But the visitor won't let himself be put off, once, just once, he would like to get to the bottom of the thing. But now it's all getting too silly for those he's interrogating. They're glad that at last, after twelve years, they have an apartment, and they've no intention whatsoever of putting what has been achieved at risk. A childish idea to kick up a row about something so trivial. Only a foreigner would think of doing that. The police would know in five minutes who was trying to hatch illegal protests here, who the ringleaders were! All right. But why not try self-help then? Get hold of a couple of shovels, a truck, lay a drain pipe perhaps, and level the entrance – it could be done in two weekends. Impossible. Gravel, pipes, building material are all state property. Private building activity in the city is prohibited. Only a fool can make the attempt to rent a truck. And anyway, how many times do we have to say it? If anything at all is going to be done, then it can only come from the top, and anyone who refuses to understand that will never understand this country. But the alternative is that the thirty families who live here will have to stumble through the mud till the end of their lives! No reply. We part, not without a certain degree of exasperation. The visitor has broken one of the rules, transgressed an unwritten law. What is self-evident to him, is unthinkable to everyone who is at home here.

## A HYPOTHESIS

Anyone who has travelled a lot can report such episodes. They are as numerous as a swarm of mosquitoes and just as difficult to chase away. The only question is where they are to be placed.

A little test is perhaps appropriate here. Anyone who wants to can place a cross by the correct locations:

|  |  |
|---|---|
| ☐ Central African Republic | ☐ China |
| ☐ Paraguay | ☐ Romania |
| ☐ Bangla Desh | ☐ Angola |
| ☐ Zaire | ☐ Cuba |

☐ Indonesia        ☐ Soviet Union
☐ Haiti             ☐ Vietnam
☐ Ethiopia       ☐ Bulgaria

True stories prove nothing. But they are very important. The Second and Third World are shockingly like one another. Their inhabitants' basic experience of society, from the miseries of everyday life to the rituals of power, are hardly any different. Instead of explaining this state of affairs, the ideologists habitually work at denying it. If an analysis is attempted at all, it goes roughly like this:

In contrast to the predictions of the classical thinkers of Marxism, the Bolsheviks and their epigones were not victorious where industrialization had advanced furthest. It was not the Western European or the North American working class which seized power; instead it was minute cadre parties who came to power in backward societies as a result of coups and civil wars, and succeeded because they were able to win over the mass of the peasantry, because they appeared as organizers of national campaigns of liberation, or because they were supported militarily by a strong occupying power. 'Victorious socialism' must therefore be understood as a direct or an indirect product of underdevelopment; analogies between conditions in Paraguay and those in Romania, similarities between Haiti and Vietnam would have to be explained in historical terms, as mere remnants of the past.

Sixty-five years after the October Revolution such an interpretation has lost much of its plausibility and it seems to me that it's time to test another, antithetical, hypothesis: perhaps it's not only the case that underdeveloped societies bring forth socialist regimes; perhaps on the contrary, socialist regimes bring forth underdeveloped social forms. Despite being so obvious, this conjecture has as yet been little discussed. I'm counting on the gratitude of my friends and enemies, if I now make a modest start. My hypothesis is: really existing socialism is the highest stage of underdevelopment.

# A DIGRESSION ON NAMES

If two children are arguing about who is to be first to press
the new plastic toy to his breast or demolish it, then it's all
the same to them whether the object of their difference of
opinion is called Super Galaxy or Space Robot Mark IV. The
more adult the disputants, however, the more importance
they place on what the thing they're fighting about is
supposed to be called. Matters can go so far that the quarrel
over words is conducted much more doggedly than that over
the realities they designate.

> 'When *I* use a word', Humpty Dumpty said, 'it means just what
> I choose it to mean – neither more nor less.' 'The question is',
> said Alice, 'whether you can make words so many different
> things.' 'The question is', said Humpty Dumpty, 'which is to be
> master – that's all.'
>
> Lewis Carroll, *Alice Through the Looking-Glass*

So it becomes a question of power whether this or that
republic is to be written with or without quotation marks or
is to be prefixed by the word so-called, whether the Falklands
are called the Malvinas or the Malvinas the Falklands; and
there doesn't even seem to be any agreement whether the
name of our own country has to be spoken in full or whether
one is allowed to abbreviate it to Bay-Air-Day [BRD, i.e.
FRG].

Now if the disputed toy has attained the size of a system
in which a third of humanity lives, then one can hardly hear
a single word one's saying for all the shouting going on. How
signifier relates to signified is a question semanticists, sema-
siologists and semioticians can be allowed to grow fat on.
Since I don't have such expertise, I shall here list only a few
of the possibilities that are available: the socialist camp, the
state trading nations, world communism, the Second World,
the state capitalist, the monopoly bureaucratic, the post-capi-
talist societies ...

All these dry-as-dust phrases are put completely in the shade by that brilliant expression which these countries, after years of searching, finally coined for themselves: that is, Really Existing Socialism.

What I like so much about this term is its involuntary content. A shop assistant would be puzzled by a customer who asked for a packet of really existing cigarettes, as would the employers' association by a trade union demanding really existing wage rises. It would also be difficult to imagine Kaiser Wilhelm II hitting on the idea of describing himself as a really existing emperor. Only someone who is prey to doubts can constantly protest that he really exists; and it's part of the underlying charm of this official linguistic invention by the party, that such doubt is only all too justified.

But at the same time, the term tells everyone who has ears to hear: Gentlemen – dissidents, foreigners, critics and grumblers, dear hostile elements! You can talk till the cows come home, just as much as you like, I am a brute fact, swallow that if you can! The use of the words, really existing socialism, is therefore simultaneously affirmative and resigned; the former in that it maintains that socialism truly exists, that the longed-for Messiah long ago came down to us; the latter because it lets us know this must suffice, there's nothing more to come: this is addressed to all those crackpots, dreamers and utopians, who have still not grasped that the Twelfth of Never of their hopes is long past.

Who would have expected such brilliance from a nameless author in the propaganda department of the Central Committee of the CPSU! If I nevertheless risk proposing an improvement to this happy invention then it's for two reasons. First, the word Socialism has an honourable past and it doesn't seem quite fair to cheat after the event all those who brought it into the world; the militant journeymen and the bearded prophets, the travelling preachers and the refugees, the generous students and the determined strike-leaders of the nineteenth century didn't choose their successors, and I don't at all see why today's oppressors should be able to enrich themselves from their legacy. And secondly, the formula of the really etc. isn't very handy. In future, therefore, I shall permit myself to call the monstrous phenomenon re-exocism [*Resozismus*], a word which, I hope, will trip much more lightly from everyone's tongue, whether friend or foe.

## BIRDS OF A FEATHER FLOCK TOGETHER

Everyone knows, or believes he knows, what underdevelopment is. But to make sure that we understand one another properly, and so that no one can pretend that he doesn't know what is meant, here is a short checklist:

*Economic condition*: Dependence on world market, limited self-sufficiency. Need to be subsidized by richer countries. Import of advanced technology, payment by export of raw materials. Growing indebtedness to capitalist suppliers, which can go so far that the underdeveloped country is technically bankrupt.

*Political system*: Extreme dominance of personality, allied with personality cult. One-party system with mafia-like characteristics. Absence of rules for succession to the leadership. Privileged position of the military and the secret police. Cold civil war. Arbitrariness of justice, total censorship, institutionalized corruption, state terrorism.

The more striking the similarities, the more important the differences are: any comparison which fails to pay attention to them won't get far.

1. Re-exocism has not simply set underdevelopment as its goal; it aims to bring about its finest flowering. The people won't starve, as in Mali or Bangla Desh. Everyone is to be fed, but badly fed; educated, but badly educated; housed, but badly housed. This goal has been reached in most re-

exocist countries and it's no small matter. But these famous re-exocist 'achievements' are also the limit of what is intended for the inhabitants of the Second World: thus far and no further. The surplus value that can be produced beyond this level, either flows into the pockets of the privileged class ('no-menklatura') or is used for armaments, the only sector which can bear comparison in every respect with its counterpart in the capitalist countries.

2. Underdevelopment is not a natural phenomenon, and it should certainly not be seen as a mere relic of the past. On the contrary, it is a product of modernization. Anyone who wants to underdevelop a country must smash the old pre-industrial society and cannibalize its components. All the 'backward' features which ease the transition from the new misery to the old will be adopted. Among the resources of the bad old, the local forms of oppression are especially important. That's why, just like classic colonialism, re-exocism draws, wherever it can, on traditional methods of domination: on Czarism in the Soviet Union, on the Prussian legacy in the GDR, on the rule of caudillos and local bosses in Latin America, and on Asiatic despotism in the Far East.

3. In classical imperialism the simple logic of exploitation dominated: the more miserable the condition of the colonies grew, the richer the metropolitan countries became. The rapid underdevelopment of the African, Asian and Latin American societies in the nineteenth century was only the reverse side of an equally rapid development of the 'mother lands'. As is well known, the 'independence' which the former colonies struggled to achieve, has not fundamentally altered this relationship.

The re-exocist camp, however, cannot point to any flourishing metropolis outside its borders. The Soviet Union produces and reproduces its own underdevelopment, under its own steam, as it were. If a corner grocery shop goes out of business, that's usually a consequence of the concentration of capital: the spoils go to the new supermarket. The bank-ruptcy of re-exocism, on the other hand, has immanent, home-grown causes. It's not just since Afghanistan and Poland that, with the best of reasons, one can talk about Soviet imperialism: yet that should not make one forget that this is an imperialism *sui generis* from which big brother benefits very little. People live considerably better in Budapest, Berlin and Prague than in Moscow, to say nothing of metropoles like Belogorsk, Ashkhabad and Namangan.

4. Where 'victorious' re-exocism meets with an already developed industrial society, endless troubles ensue. The difficulties begin with the seizure of power. A spontaneous popular vote for re-exocism, whether by election or revolt, is unthinkable; the system can only be imposed by a *coup d'état* or by military power. But even where this has succeeded, as in Poland, in Czechoslovakia, in Hungary and in East Germany, the victors' real task is still to come: a forced regression to the Soviet level. However, it is far from easy permanently to suppress the productive energies of an advanced society. Two possibilities are available to the hegemonic power in order to establish re-exocism, the highest stage of underdevelopment: it can attempt to skim off the excess surplus value through 'economic co-operation', that is, through unequal agreements; or, where this leads to rebellions, it can lend 'fraternal aid'. Nevertheless it has still not succeeded in bringing about Mongolian conditions in the GDR or Hungary.

## SCAPEGOATS

There are many theories of underdevelopment. Almost all of them seek their explanations in material facts, in the analysis of economic processes. Now it is true that re-exocist regimes are distinguished by a high demand for theory; but they refuse to apply any of these theories to themselves. That's not so much due to the content of the theories as to the fact that in the eyes of re-exocists, re-exocism is immune to theory from the very start. For according to them there can be no yardstick against which their actions could be measured. Their own theory, known as dialectical materialism, appears to them least of all suited to this purpose. This has the curious result that – by comparison with Nicolae Ceausescu and Fidel Castro – the Agnellis and Rockefellers, the Flicks and the MacNamaras appear as the true materialists simply because they are used to measuring the success of economic activities by the economic results which they produce. The leaders of re-exocism, by contrast, are extreme idealists since they refuse any test of reality on principle.

Under these circumstances the question naturally arises, who or what is to be answerable for their failures. The answer was settled a good half century ago. It's the fault of (a) the enemy, (b) the past, and (c) human fallibility.

Re-exocism has the peculiar habit of portraying itself simultaneously as invincible champion and injured innocence. On the one hand it is eternally victorious, on the other it suffers from the malevolence of its internal and external enemies. Where the dark plots of capitalists, the machinations of reactionary forces don't provide enough cover, then, if necessary, the inner enemy is produced. That this enemy has to be eliminated immediately is self-evident. However, as a result of successful liquidation a gap appears which has to be filled by new definitions of the enemy and so on. Although its opponents are required in order to excuse failure, re-exocism regards itself as the innocent victim. Re-exocism is like a boxer who is never tired of complaining about the existence of other boxers; if only these troublemakers disappeared then he would be world champion.

Re-exocist propaganda refers with similar insight to the evil past, the impossible legacy which it had to take over. To that legacy belongs, above all, the old Adam, a creature which is evidently difficult to eradicate. Here the rhetoric of justification follows the simple before-and-after model familiar from old shampoo or deodorant advertisements. The disadvantage of this method is that it only works in the short term. If the miracle ingredient still isn't working after sixty-five years, a certain scepticism spreads even among idiots.

A third possibility for the assignment of guilt is the ritual of self-criticism. What the repentant scapegoat comes up with, even if he is shot on the basis of his statement (which nowadays only rarely happens), is always only a sham confession. 'Comrades, I have made mistakes. I feel remorse. It will never happen again.' With that, the problem is localized once and for all in the scapegoat's breast and the system can pass on to the rest of the agenda. Once upon a time, there was a theory called Marxism. The invocation of 'mistakes', which provide excuses instead of analyses, is its most extreme negation.

## SUMMARY OF A DISASTER

Difficult to say where underdevelopment begins, and where it leads. I admit that. One can plough through production and trade statistics as long as one likes and study the thickest tomes of the historians and political scientists without getting to the bottom of the matter. Because it isn't simply an economic and political phenomenon; it affects life as a whole, it's a disaster which penetrates into every last corner and crevice of social and individual existence. Someone who isn't subject to it himself will never quite understand its dark secrets; and if one does not wish to remain completely ignorant then one must consult its greatest writers, turn to the stories of V.S. Naipaul and Andrei Platanov, of Salman Rushdie and Gabriel García Márquez. In comparison with what they have to tell us, every attempt from the outside to understand underdevelopment as an anthropological category remains schematic and abstract; so, too, the following summary which is intended to draw together some of the grave and typical consequences of underdevelopment through re-exocism.

*Lack and waste* exist everywhere, and the one is everywhere related to the other in some subterranean way. Even where great wealth is the rule, misery feeds on extravagance and vice versa, as we know only too well. However, where the society as a whole is poor, the antagonism takes murderous forms. While the tractors stand idle because yet again there are no spare parts, women queue for bread in the towns; machine tools imported for hard currency rust on the quayside; unusable goods are produced by the ton, but there are no lightbulbs for months on end. Absurd promises for the distant future, which no one believes, are supposed to substitute for daily milk. Grandiose plans are proclaimed and work on them begun when everyone who possesses even a trace of expertise knows that they are impracticable. The indifference, the red tape and the incompetence of an all-powerful bureaucracy are not beyond description, but only very good writers should attempt the task. Only someone who never contradicts anything has a chance of rising in the apparatus. The negative selection is remorseless, the corruption endemic, the waste of resources never-ending.

*Worthlessness of time.* Since there is no project that appears to make a way out possible, the subject population sees no reason for collective effort. Slave morality makes a permanent passive strike a duty. The whole pace of life slows down. In every one of the countless offices that have to be attended one learns that time is worth nothing; it's necessary to queue three times to buy a pair of trousers, once to find out if there are any trousers, a second time to pay for the trousers, a third time for them to be handed over. Billions of working hours are lost through this stupid ritual, that has been practised for decades; the productivity of agriculture as of industry remains pitifully low.

*Disinformation.* In underdeveloped societies the circulation of information is seriously impeded. The population is at the mercy of the crude propaganda of the media. Government co-ordination and censorship ensure that most news only circulates in the form of rumours. Otherwise access to information is strictly dependent on position in the social hierarchy. To that extent the leadership enjoys a monopoly of information which is further amplified by the manic secretiveness which is evident everywhere. The ruling clique tries to gain an overview of what is happening in society through a systematic network of spies. However, the policeman is overstretched as an 'intellectual collective worker'; his cognitive potential necessarily lags behind that of society as a whole.

The interruption of communication, however, also has disagreeable consequences for the leadership, because every form of self-regulation is suppressed. The economic results have often been described. Since regulation by the market is absent, prices are fixed administratively without reference to costs: demand plays no determining role for production. But this is only one aspect of a degeneration which encompasses every aspect of life. Since all *feedback* 'from below' is choked off, the leadership can congratulate itself with a flood of success stories. They never stop. Therefore a 'mistaken' decision must always assume vast dimensions before it is noticed; only then does the leadership become aware of it and change course, i.e. prepare its next mistake. It's obvious that the learning ability of such a system is minimal.

*Regression.* Every day the citizens of an underdeveloped country are confronted yet again with their defenceless exposure to arbitrary power, repression and bureaucratic slovenliness. Awareness of their impotence leads to resignation, to withdrawal into an extremely restricted private sphere, to political apathy. All that counts is to scrape through, to avoid making decisions, to practise mimicry and to refrain from any criticism or initiative.

*Inability to innovate.* Muscles that are never used atrophy. In the long term, underdevelopment causes its victims to forget how to produce something new. Not even in the armaments sector, on which it bestows so much love, has re-exocism managed to invent anything fundamentally new; in every other area it is content to imitate whatever developed societies have to offer.

Inevitably, it has not produced any original culture either. Artistic production either falls back on pre-industrial remains (folklore), or it follows, with epigonal delay, the models of the Western metropolis.

*An illusion backed by force.* Re-exocism as the highest stage of underdevelopment has made heroic efforts in order to repress the feeling that it has brought nothing but misfortune to the subjected peoples. Envy and the resentment of failure stamp its official statements, which fluctuate between megalomania and self-pity. It has made the Potemkin village a central principle of its self-presentation. It replies to the total scepticism of the population with illusions backed up by force. At the pinnacle of its hierarchies cynicism and paranoia merge to form an indissoluble mass. Underdevelopment gives birth to delusion. Re-exocism elevates it to a system.

## ENVOI

I admit that these reflections are one-sided. I admit that it's difficult to say something 'objective' about underdevelopment. I even admit that one can also find good sides to it. There are people among us – we all know them – who believe they can rediscover things in poor societies that we have lost: elementary experiences, mutual help, slow Sundays, unselfish feelings, work in the fields, equality in common adversity. What they dislike are the very things that give us an advantage. The complexity of our lives is too much for them, the coldness and the injustice of our struggles repels them, the prospect of future catastrophes alarms them, their complaints about 'emptiness' and 'meaninglessness' have been getting on our nerves for some time now. I admit that there is some truth to their complaints, even if they express them badly and clumsily. But this truth only concerns us. It says nothing about the Second, Third, Fourth World. What the searchers after meaning believe they can discover there is nothing more than a projection of their own problems. They're like the six blind men of Hindustan describing an elephant. Such yearning doesn't mean much to me. The Poles aren't a tribe of Indians, the Cubans are not Anabaptists. Nowhere, from Managua to Shanghai, can even the faintest reflection of earlier revolutions be sighted today. The destruction of human desires, human imagination, human productivity on a massive scale: anyone who believes underdevelopment by force is a solution, is seeking his salvation in a delusion.

*(1982)*

# 4

# A Determined Effort to Explain to a

# New York Audience the Secrets of

# German Democracy

You are surprised, ladies and gentlemen, at much of what you have heard from West Germany of late; and because you would like to know how things stand with regard to liberty and social control, to the democratic rule of law, and police repression in that part of the world, have invited me here. I am grateful to you for the interest you take in the conditions in which we find ourselves, for the more concerned you are about them the better. The Federal Republic is dependent on America. After all we are a protectorate of the United States even if it is not considered good taste to discuss this subject publicly. A single critical word spoken here in New York has, for that reason, more weight than a collection of twenty thousand signatures in Lower Saxony or West Berlin. Getting out of a plane in Hamburg or Munich you will observe that German society, thirty-five years after the end of the Nazi tyranny, makes a thoroughly civilized impression. In general you need not be afraid that you will be shouted at. In the tax offices and in the banks you will meet long-haired, casually dressed young people just like in New York or anywhere else. No one stands to attention. A certain courtesy is displayed. The officers of the armed forces do not look as if they were called Erich von Stroheim. In the government offices you will be met with affability – unless you happen to be a Turk or a Communist – and sometimes even then. German democracy, you will perhaps say, is a success – and you will find yourselves confirmed in that opinion when you read our constitution. For it is a very splendid constitution and it is by no means a dead letter; on the contrary, on all sides people struggle – one can only say madly – to fulfil it. Newspapers and politicians' speeches are full of it; the word 'constitution' is one of the commonest German words. You may know that our language inclines to compounds and so our constitution forms part of the most varied verbal combinations. In our country people constantly speak about protection of the constitution, loyalty to the constitution, complaints under the constitution, enemies of the constitution, consonance with the constitution, incompatibility with the constitution.

So much zeal may astonish you and you will wonder since when Germans have felt so strongly about democracy. Well, apart from isolated, courageous but quickly frustrated attempts to implement it in the nineteenth century, our country has not much experience of this form of state. The Weimar Republic lasted only fourteen years and how precarious that short life was is common knowledge. But our present basic law came into existence under the occupation of the victorious allies – malicious people have even maintained that democracy was imposed on the Germans as a punishment for losing the war. But this external pressure cannot explain why it has established itself in the course of the last decades and why it has become pleasingly familiar to the West Germans. Over and above the precursors already mentioned, Germany's strong federal traditions have no doubt played a part. But above all the political and economic requirements of the reconstruction period favoured the growth of democracy. The Federal Republic required widely scattered, decentralized initiatives, integration with Western Europe, membership of the world market, dissipation of the suspicion of Fascism, mobility and the unhindered flow of information. Under the pressure of external and internal conditions the old-fashioned authoritarian state had to give way. If you give a child a toy and after a time try to take it away again you must be prepared for unexpectedly strong resistance. That is the case today with many German politicians – in fact it is worse, for that considerable section of the population which was able, over several decades, to convince itself of the advantages of democracy is not content simply to defend its rights. In the sixties we saw something like a democratic offensive; in fact the point was reached where a West German head of government allowed himself to go so far as to utter the programmatic statement that the time had come 'to risk more democracy'.

If, however, you read our press today you will take your head in your hands. Not a day goes by without a horrific infringement by government departments, without a scandalous judgement in the courts, without a ruse by the police; and on our television you can see and hear politicians who find not only democracy but the very thought of it unbearable, indeed incomprehensible. They even insist on going on record to that effect in speeches and interviews. You will ask yourselves: What is all this? How does all this hang together? The question is fully justified; I put it to myself daily. For the time being only one thing is clear among all these contradictions. Anyone who attempts to explain the Federal Republic to himself or to others finds himself in a cognitive dilemma. What does an intellectual do then in such a case? He tries to construct a theory or at least to form a hypothesis. Admittedly in so doing he must make an assumption which is not entirely to be taken for granted. He must act, that is to say, as if the social conditions which have to be explained added up, so to speak, and are not completely irrational. I don't need to tell you how risky such an assumption is. I shall make it, however, but only for the sake of argument, as a joke as it were, and without real conviction. In this connection two reservations require to be made.

The first concerns the division of Germany. I cannot report on circumstances in the eastern half of the country and do not wish to do so. It seems to me to be superfluous in our context, for the German Democratic Republic is not a democratic state. From the first, it has consistently denied its inhabitants the civic rights and freedoms we are discussing here. The government party which has had power since the founding of the GDR has never allowed the slightest doubt about that. It is true that the East German state possesses a written constitution; it also stages certain democratic rituals at regular intervals, such as general elections and ceremonial sittings of the People's Chamber, which is the simulacrum of a parliament; but the Stalin Constitution of 1936 in the USSR, among others, has given us illuminating examples of how little the existence of such documents and institutions means. Anyway that is simply not the object of the exercise. If the East Germans are pursuing any goal at all with their constitution it has so far escaped me. My friends in East Berlin maintain that it is a case of a kind of black humour with which the regime cheers itself up at their expense. I am inclined to doubt that; for in my country people either have power or a sense of humour but never both together.

I do not intend to say that East Germany is run in an entirely arbitrary fashion. The opposite is the case. Society in the GDR is distinguished by an extreme degree of careful regulation. A highly developed system of rules and provisions protects the population from social and economic risks; at the same time it ensures that fundamental rights, such as freedom of movement, freedom of association, and freedom of the press, are abolished with painstaking thoroughness and remain so. That is well known to every German, however stupid and clueless he may otherwise be, and it would be superfluous to waste words on the subject if there were not people in West Germany who, on the one hand, are firm supporters of the GDR and, on the other, display a peculiar zeal when it comes to fighting against the 'demolition of democratic rights' in West Germany. These people are an unhappy spectacle. I find their attitude theoretically inconsistent and morally intolerable.

I shall therefore confine myself to the Federal Republic of Germany. But even where the country I live in is concerned you must not demand too much of me. The American media – above all the *New York Times* – has for the last ten years fairly consistently spared you news about the reverses which democracy has suffered in Germany during that time. Perhaps it did not wish to upset the cordial understanding between the governments of our two countries. I would not know how to attempt to make up for the omission in half an hour. The complaints book from which I should have to read would be too thick for that. Besides, anyone, no matter from what part of the world he came, could produce similar rosaries of indignation; you as Americans have plenty of practice at it. The result of such a recital would be familiar to you. It would have little effect. I therefore want to attempt something else: I should like, as well as I can, to recapitulate for you the bitter public debate which has been conducted for several years on our subject.

First, I shall briefly introduce to you the two parties who engage in it. On the one side is the chequered coalition of those who find the increasing state repression unacceptable: old anti-fascists, who have drawn basic moral lessons from the horrors of German history; liberals who take their convictions more seriously than is usual with liberals; Christian groups who protest against the increase in state repression on the grounds of conscience; but above all a series of endlessly splintered and feuding 'movements', which all have their origins in the anti-authoritarian movement of 1967/68 – especially women, ecologists, the old New Left and the new New Left, as well as a fairly amorphous mass of young people who have turned away shrugging their shoulders, sickened by the official lie: all in all, a minority millions strong, which, just as in the United States, forms a complicated patchwork of opposition. Although it is held together neither by a theory nor by an organization, indeed perhaps for that very reason, the politicians fear it as the devil fears holy water. For this minority is vociferous, determined and difficult to crucify. And I do not believe that it can be silenced in the foreseeable future.

On the other side in this conflict you will find those forces which in Germany are described as supportive of the state and which consider themselves to be such, although up to now they have ruined one German political system after another. To these forces the overwhelming majority of our political class belong – that is to say, the cadres controlled by the parliamentary parties and the state apparatus.

With such a distribution of roles it is no wonder that, while debate is carried on angrily and without quarter, the arguments are of paralysing monotony. The galloping modernization of

Germany came to a halt at the political sphere. Here we find ourselves, as ever, involved in conflicts which stem from the year 1848. That is what is so barren and anachronistic about our fights – that they must be conducted as if we still had a bourgeois revolution to come, although the militant bourgeoisie which would be necessary for it has long since ceased to exist.

All right – I shall recapitulate. First of all what one side says. Since 1968, they say, the state based on the rule of law has constantly lost ground. Parties and governments, the courts and big business have reacted to the shock of the student movement and the signs of crisis in the economy with a massive roll-back operation, which has recourse to the old arsenal of right-wing, if not Fascist, ideologies. The democratic rights guaranteed by the constitution are slowly but surely being liquidated and the point in time is approaching when we shall once more find ourselves in those disagreeable circumstances which we know from our history: with an authoritarian state; with blind obedience; with the persecution of minorities; with general social regression. We have already seen the *Berufsverbot* in action (they say), the drafting of a police law which legalizes execution on the public thoroughfare as 'shooting in self-defence', the buggings and provocations by the secret service, the intimidation and harassment of defence lawyers, and direct and indirect censorship in the schools, universities and media.

Nonsense. Absolute rubbish. A slander on the Federal Republic, shouts the other side – the Federal government, the leader writers, the public prosecutors. West German society, they say, is, with all its defects, more democratic, more free and tolerant than any earlier one to exist on our soil. Open and blunt criticism on every newspaper stand; as much Marx and Engels in the University as you could wish for; travel all over the world; enlightened teachers and pupils, parents and children; information for anyone that wants it; grants for artists who gnaw away at the status quo; and reform after reform. How many nations are there in the world today, they ask, which can demonstrate such a degree of democratic maturity? The list, they reply, would be short. You would find Holland on it, Great Britain (but not

Northern Ireland), a couple of Scandinavian countries and perhaps the United States ... Admittedly, they say, we have unfortunately had to take certain steps in order to preserve this model state of affairs; but for that we deserve to be praised not criticized. In the Federal Republic at least four thousand agents from the GDR are at work as well as an unknown number of terrorists, who have openly declared that they intend to destroy our democracy by all possible means. The vast majority of our fellow-citizens, they say, expect and demand of us that we protect the Federal Republic from these attacks and these dangers.

The two pleas from which I have given you extracts are wonderfully to the point and enlightening. It is actually their greatest virtue that they are so comprehensible. You will perhaps be surprised if I tell you that I cannot come down on the side of either. In these hand-painted little woodcuts I do not recognize the reality of a country which is swarming with the most absurd contradictions. Admittedly, given my experience of life and my temperament, I entirely incline towards democracy and that has always meant in Germany to the radical opposition. I have after all had my house searched a few times; my telephone has been tapped for months if not for years; and at the end of the sixties and the beginning of the seventies I got to know the gentlemen in plain clothes who sat in front of my house in a little Volkswagen so well that I was tempted to ask them for a light when I was out of matches. I mention that only so that you do not think of me as a naive liberal if I confess to you that I may be annoyed daily at German idiosyncrasies but I am not afraid. I do not feel threatened. I see no reason to panic. So far I have not been taken to court for any of my publications. It is true that West German television refuses my collaboration but occasionally allows me to have my say in an interview. For ten years I have been editing a periodical the contents of which would have landed me in prison in the kind of political conditions which were considered normal in Germany for hundreds of years. Since it was founded in 1965 it has only once been taken to court – a fine. Not one number has so far been confiscated. That might naturally be because it is considered innocuous. Or else we have simply been lucky. I know a fair number of editors, authors and printers, who have had different experiences; many of them are still in prison.

I should also not like to conceal the fact that work like ours can bring unpleasant surprises in its wake. Several years ago we published a number the main theme of which was the position of political prisoners in the Federal Republic. Shortly after it was distributed there was an incident. My publishing partner, Karl Markus Michel, was sitting at his desk one evening when there was a loud ring at the door bell. Michel opened the door and found himself confronted by a group of heavies who demanded that he should at once withdraw the number from circulation; they also demanded that the publishers pay a fine. They threatened to take his house apart and beat him to pulp but after a while went away without doing anything. It emerged from the argument that these people considered themselves to be sympathizers of the Red Army Faction.

Two years later Michel – who could describe his amazement! – was wakened at about six in the morning by an unusual noise. Someone was breaking down his front door. Seconds later four men had surrounded his bed and Michel saw the muzzles of their machine pistols aimed at him. Unlike a Scotsman by the name of MacLeod who lived in Stuttgart at the time and who obviously did not have strong enough nerves to live in Germany – he was shot dead through his door by secret police who mistakenly thought he was a terrorist because he refused to open up – Michel had the presence of mind not to blink an eyelid. The gentlemen eventually informed him that they belonged to the Bonn security group, a section of the Federal Criminal Agency, and proceeded to search his house, in the course of which they leafed through every book in Michel's library – a considerable undertaking with nine thousand books. The tone of voice which the visitors adopted was markedly polite and with the passage of time even became solicitous. They apologized – the front door had almost opened by itself. Admittedly his wife – like many other women citizens of Frankfurt – was arrested and held in prison for weeks in the course of this operation (it was called

Winter Journey) on the suspicion of founding or supporting a criminal organization (article 219 of the Criminal Code). She was not brought to trial. To compensate for this, the visit of the gentlemen from the Federal Criminal Agency was repeated a year and a half later – another break-in, another house search. Four years later the proceedings under article 219 were quietly dropped. This story is so unexceptional that most German papers did not think it necessary to report it.

In the years that have passed since then neither Michel nor his wife has had any trouble with the police. They simply get on with their work as if nothing had happened – and nothing has happened. The Minister of the Interior who was responsible for the break-in to Michel's house – he is called Maihofer – later had to take his leave because of an excessively flagrant breach of the constitution. Incidentally he belongs to the Free Democratic Party, which maintains that it is the guardian of liberty in Germany. I read recently that Herr Maihofer has got a chair at the University of Constance. No doubt he will lecture there on the democratic state and the rule of law and occasionally meet Michel on the campus; he often goes to Constance to talk to contributors to our periodical.

Herr Baum, who succeeded Herr Maihofer as Minister of the Interior, was recently kind enough to invite me to dinner in Bonn. Presumably the Minister was not familiar with my police dossier. I have not had the opportunity to read it either but with a little help from my friends, as the song says, I learn that it is amazingly full. My friends who have studied it came to the conclusion that the political police is the victim of a number of illusions as far as I am concerned. None of these errors seems meantime to threaten my life.

Now I would not like to maintain that the stories I have told you can simply be generalized; but one thing, I think, does emerge from them. The political reality which we are dealing with is a mess. To convey to you what goes on in the heads of the people who rule West Germany is an impossible task. One gets the impression that they are fairly confused. I have given some thought to this problem and even if I cannot claim to have found a solution – I doubt that such a solution exists – I should nevertheless like to risk a hypothesis for discussion in the hope that it may cast a little light on the secrets with which we are surrounded. I maintain therefore that in the Federal Republic two historically and structurally quite different systems of repression exist side by side – that each system has its own logic and that these logics are not reconcilable. All they have in common is the mad idea of perfect 'internal security'.

The first system of repression we have inherited from our ancestors – a legacy that no one is likely to envy us. Its origins lie in the early nineteenth century; Metternich and Bismarck were its first masters. Hitler brought it to monstrous flowering; Adenauer saved what could be saved from its ruins. Its political basis was the authoritarian state; its equivalent in terms of foreign policy imperialist expansion by military means. In the postwar years it has lost prestige but its supporters, who are all to be numbered among the extreme Right, defend it with bulldoglike tenacity.

The second system of surveillance and repression, on the other hand, is a genuine product of the post-Second World War period. It is designed for the historically new requirements of the Federal Republic. Its domestic political basis is the integration of the working class by means of mass consumption and the welfare state; its foreign political equivalent is the offensive of the German export economy in the world market.

The older system was deeply rooted in the particular development of our country and had markedly chauvinistic traits; the more recent one is entirely international. In its attitudes it is just about as primitively German as IBM. I can still remember very clearly the political police with whom we had to deal in 1968. They had no idea of the history of the workers' movement and believed in all seriousness that anyone who demonstrated was 'in the pay of Moscow'. Many of them suffered from a pronounced weapon fetishism; an obscure mixture of fear, resentment, prejudice and paranoia were the constituents of their unconscious drives. They were attached to their own delusions, which they used to call their *Weltanschauung*, with a kind of passion. There were many racists among them. You could gather from their remarks that they detested foreigners, Jews, communists, people with long hair, gays, artists and intellectuals. They responded to critical arguments of any kind with amazement and unbelievable anger. Their ideas about the reality outside their offices were hazy and their mode of thinking was characterized by symbolism rather than analysis. To that extent it is not surprising that the operations of these guardians of law and order were so disastrous that the government was concerned about their adverse effect on public opinion abroad. This kind of servant of the state has, unfortunately, not died out even today. The traditional forms of repression may be antiquated but there is in our political establishment one wing that defends it stubbornly; in the main, it is the right wing of the CDU/CSU represented by people like Dr Strauss, Dr Stoltenberg and Dr Filbinger. If you have not heard of these people so much the better for you.

Now for the more progressive experts in control and repression of a kind that we encounter with increasing frequency. They are by type technocrats, have almost always been through college and usually have a fairly sophisticated view of the world. Many of them even see themselves as scientists. Rational discourse and analysis are not unfamiliar to them and in general they have no interest in cloudy *Weltanschauungen*. Today there are policemen in the Federal Republic who carry out comparative studies of ideological systems like botanists classifying plants. A real pro of this kind will try to go about things without prejudice. He is even ready to co-operate with communists if he sees advantage in it. His only obsession is security; he understands thereby the need to see that everything that functions should continue to function. That is naturally a very ambitious aim. To attain it the experts must foresee and eliminate every imaginable malfunction, no matter what causes them or what their motivation may be. He cherishes no special hatred for intellectuals, if only because he counts himself among their number; indeed he sees in them a very promising field for recruitment. The past hardly interests him; he considers himself orientated towards the future. His political home is usually Social Democracy but occasionally also the Liberal Party. An exceptional example of this type is Dr Herold, the head of the West German Federal Criminal Bureau.

His power does not come from the barrel of a gun but from the software of his computer. From his forty-million-mark headquarters in Wiesbaden he rules over the most modern police data-processing system in the world. From this operations centre he has immediate access to the computers of the provincial Criminal Bureaux, of the Customs Service, of the border guards, of the offices of the judiciary and the prison system, of the central Federal registry, of the documentation system JURIS, to the computers of the state prosecutors and the data network of Interpol; over and above that – thanks to 'departmental co-operation' (which in German means the exchange of information between officials in different spheres, exchanges which are short-circuits not individually based on legality) – he has access to the data banks of the vehicle licensing offices, of the aliens register, of local registration offices, of the tax offices, social services offices, health offices, of the building authorities, of libraries, of the Federal insurance bureau, military security, the Federal intelligence services, and the Federal Agency for the Defence of the Constitution.* I apologize for that long sentence. Its syntax merely reflects the tangled undergrowth of our bureaucracies.

Moreover the use of data by the police reaches far into what are supposedly 'private' areas. Informally the booking systems to hotels, car-hire firms, airlines, travel agencies, estate agents, pawnbrokers and credit inquiry offices are tapped. All this storage of information is conducted on the principle: record as much as possible, never delete anything. The laws restricting access to data, which have been announced in the last few years, allow these practices that they claim to restrict by means of generous exceptions to the rule; they are window-dressing. The dimensions of the operation and of the planning in West Germany is demonstrated by the fact that one sub-system – it is

---

*The political police. [Tr.]

called INPOL – carries out some two million transactions daily
for its own use alone, over a 60,000 kilometre network. It is certain
that the population of West Germany is subject to a degree of
surveillance without precedent in history. The Gestapo could
only dream of technical means of these dimensions. In the foreseeable future, Dr Herold and his colleagues will probably be in
the position to follow all our movements on their monitors if they
feel like so doing. When you present your passport at a West
German airport it is laid on a glass plate. The video terminal that
reads it is connected to a central computer. But also when you
spend a night in a hotel, borrow a book or visit your dentist, you
leave behind a permanent trace.

An interesting contrast to Dr Herold's bomb-proof concrete
fortress in Wiesbaden is presented by the central office for tracing
Nazi criminals at Ludwigsburg. I once had occasion to look up
the register that is kept there. No trace of Orwellian perfection.
The index of names consists of around 100,000 sheets covered
with handwritten scribbles. There is no prospect of a computer
being installed; a couple of badly paid office workers do the
whole job.

Dr Herold and his colleagues are simply more interested in the
future than in the past. Their ambition extends far beyond mere
repression to the preventive planning of a cybernetically
controlled society without breakdowns. In this context the police
– on the grounds of its privileged access to information – is given
the role of a central research and development apparatus, which
acts as an early warning system, discovers defects and plans political strategies. The policeman sees himself as doing basic
research and as a social scientist, who on the basis of empirically
acquired data 'plays through' in advance on a mathematical simu-
lation model the totality of the social process, tracks down those
elements which imperil security and eliminates them before they
can emerge on a mass basis. Criminality in this context is no
longer his main opponent; he conceives of it rather as an indispensable indicator of a trend, the signals of which he has to 'eval-
uate'. I find nothing specifically German in the project.

Analogous methods of social control are being developed in all advanced countries in the West, for example in Sweden, and in Great Britain, where a research team under the direction of Sir Norman Lindop recently produced a report which corresponds with my picture down to individual details. The same holds good for the United States with this difference, that there daily life is less highly controlled by the state; as a result important surveillance networks controlled by private interests are being developed; in this connection a key role is played by the credit system.

The peculiarly German flavour, the penetrating national aroma, which characterizes the repressive measures in the Federal Republic – think only of the *Berufsverbot* or the general hysteria about terrorism – are explained, I believe, by the superimposition of old and new methods. The resulting interference is hardly likely to lead – in terms of the defenders of law and order – to the achievement of success; above all it leads to breakdowns and contradictions. It also confuses the radical–democratic opposition, whose rhetoric is fixated on its own tradition and that of its opponents. The Left is more concerned with pigs of the old school, of the kind that has been described over and over again from Heine to Tucholsky, than with Dr Herold and his colleagues at home and abroad. The good old policeman with his truncheon is easier to understand and can be opposed with simpler means than his successor.

What is disturbing about the technocrats of repression is first and foremost their learning capability, their flexibility. An occasional tactical withdrawal is nothing to them; when, for instance, it turned out that the so-called 'decrees concerning radicals' paid no dividends politically a cosmetic cover-up was employed; checking reading matter for the journey at the frontier does not seem to have paid off very well either. The traditional German chief of police, tormented by arrogance and desire for revenge, obsessed by the fear of losing face, would have obstinately blocked such learning processes. I can imagine the technocrats' complacent shrug on the day that the *Berufsverbot* is suspended – should we ever live to see that day; for they were basically never worried about the couple of thousand worthy comrades from the DKP turned down in the process but were concerned with the dossiers of the millions upon millions of people processed – dossiers which have lain in the magnetic storage systems ever since.

But there is another much more fundamental reason why it is more difficult to come to grips with the progressive system of social control than with its predecessor. The reason is that it enjoys the passive, and even in part the active, support of the massive majority of our population. This mass basis rests quite simply on the enormous success of the Federal Republic, a success which the Left has from the start denied or perhaps has not even noticed, although like everyone else they experienced it directly. It has made all Germans – even the poor – its participants and accomplices regardless of the catastrophes, crises and damage with which it is inextricably bound up. No one can escape from this success, which is chiefly but not exclusively economic in nature. In the Federal Republic power is not legitimized by any 'values' but through the way daily life functions and by the organization of survival. Consequently repression and control take on quite new features. They no longer need – or no longer exclusively need – to appeal to the unconscious, to resentment, racial hatred or chauvinism in order to divert the anger of the oppressed by projection; instead they direct everyone's attention to his own self-interest, which may be short-term but nevertheless corresponds to reality. Delusions of the kind traditionally indispensable for German politics – like anti-Semitism or the consciousness of a national mission – recede and give way to egotistical calculation.

Everyone who gets on to a plane has an immediate interest that the machine should not be hijacked or blown up; he will therefore accept the security checks and even welcome them. The gurus of the progressive police generalize this model. They place little store by the mobilization of enthusiastic masses, such as Fascism needed; they merely urge us to be 'sensible'. The civilization on which our continued existence depends, they say, is extremely complicated and very vulnerable. Its success is bought at the price of risks that increase daily: crimes, crises of scarcity, sabotage, wildcat strikes, psychological disturbances, environmental pollution, radioactive poisoning, drug addiction, economic crises, terrorism, and so on and so forth. We do not dream of contesting this. On the contrary we draw your attention to it. We ask for understanding on your part. In return we promise to obviate these dangers so far as is in our power; we offer you the maximum of security. If you don't want to be blown up you must accept our control system. A large majority of all citizens is prepared for this – at least so long as they are not directly and physically affected by the police measures. The loss of a sacrosanct private sphere is accepted and the surveillance agency can, without encountering massive resistance, prepare and store data on an entire population which 'after all has nothing to hide'.

The classical form of repression was never able to enjoy such wide support. Police power, when it shows itself brutally and without concealment on the streets, always has a polarizing effect; it musters millions of men and women against itself and gives rise to deeply rooted, continuing conflicts. Its logic is that of latent civil war. The new 'scientific' methods of social control aim, on the other hand, at integration; they are too clinical, too unbloody, to arouse mass feelings like hatred and solidarity. The megabits of information which flow hour by hour into a central computer, imperceptibly and noiselessly, provoke no tumults; they merely ensure, after all, that payments are made regularly and that the money you hand out for your sleeping tablets can be got back from the health authorities.

In a community organized on this basis, things cannot be very healthy for the bourgeois freedoms which the bourgeois state, based on the rule of law, once promised. What remains of them cannot be valued too highly nor too fiercely defended; for what remains is considerable. It makes it possible to live in the Federal Republic. I have absolutely no desire to paint conditions in my country as black. That is not only unnecessary, it would also be perverse. Such deep feelings as despair or hope would, if you ask me, be wasted on phenomena like Dr Herold. Anyone who wishes to understand his project and to estimate its chances of success must have resort to a capability which many of my friends on the Left have understandably lost the use of; he needs for his task a grim sense of humour.

When one thinks that the old and honourable European tradition of utopian thought has almost entirely died out in our day and that none of our philosophers dares any more to draw up and propose a model of a future society, then it sounds like a bad joke that it is the police who are the last to work on a Great Model. They wish to present us with a New Atlantis of universal Internal Security, a social democratic Heliopolis, an island fortress for social automats, led and directed by the omniscient and enlightened high priest in Wiesbaden. This idea is not merely macabre; it is also ridiculous. Like other and more laudable dreams of mankind, Dr Herold's utopia will come to a bad end. Presumably it will not be organized protest that will reduce his stronghold but a mightier power – erosion with its four slow, irresistible riders called laughter, muddle, accident and entropy.

(*1979*)

# 5

## Ungovernability:

## Notes from the Chancellor's Office

*Tuesday.* The boss was insufferable again today. No one can do a thing right for him. He gets more irritable every day. It's like an infectious disease: recently even I've been thinking more and more often of throwing the whole thing in, and withdrawing for some rest cure. I could do with it. A very well-run place in the Eifel Hills has been recommended to me, 4,800 DM a month, therapy and VAT included. Or it could be one of those Indian meditation centres for all I care. The main thing is to get away from here. But Monika D., the big blonde in the Procurement Section advised me against it. 'Why do you want to go to another madhouse? At least here, where you know all the other patients, your internal security is taken care of.' Worth bearing in mind. But the office atmosphere is terrible.

Today the boss already had an exchange with L. early in the morning, that could be heard in the anteroom. 'More than anything else, I'd personally like to tie a millstone round his neck and throw him in the Rhine! Drowning is all he deserves!' I don't know who they were talking about, either Haig or the Economics Minister. L. was speechless and looked pale as he left the office.

It doesn't mean very much because the old man abuses anything and anyone without inhibition. No one dares to tell him the latest unemployment figures. When the telex from Nürnberg comes, the secretary tiptoes in and lays it surreptitiously on the table. He reads far fewer documents than he used to, 'doesn't want to know all the details'.

In the evening, Lily: 'I don't understand you. Why do you put up with it all?' Etc., etc.

*Wednesday.* Tirade against the parliamentary party: muddle, lack of discipline, they all do what they like. 'It's easy enough to say take drastic action – but how?' Then on top of that there's the ministers of agriculture, the party donations scandal, the wage partners ('I only need to hear the words wage partners! Wage hyenas is what they are,') and the African heads of government, one a week on average, and each one wants a hundred million.

He also suffers like a dog from all the so-called private suppers W. has forced him to. One week it's some people from the film industry, the next week it's the railwaymen's turn, and this evening he's got to chat to a gang of scientists, biochemistry, plasma physics, cancer research, etc. I can't judge what every one of them is up to, of course, but my nose tells me: every one a charlatan. At thirty perhaps they were still doing research into something, but once their hair begins to turn grey they either become garrulous or turn religious, and I'll bet three months' salary that over dessert they're guaranteed to get round to talking about funding, medium-term funding and funding tied to particular projects, task-oriented funding and supplementary funding ...

*Thursday.* The boss arrived noticeably late today. From the anteroom I learn that supper with the scientists is supposed to have been protracted until two o'clock in the morning. I can't with the best will in the world imagine what they could have had to talk about for so long. Just before twelve the old man has me called in: 'Cancel everything for this afternoon.' – 'Out of the question.' – 'Then H. can preside. And the car at half past three, but unobtrusively.' Unbelievable. He's arranged a meeting with one of these medicine men, a certain Schack from Göttingen. Theoretical biology, whatever that might mean. As if we didn't have any other problems!

I immediately rang State Secretary K. in the Research Ministry. 'Schack? Of course I know him. High flier, Max Planck Institute, Cambridge and Stanford before that. Theory of evolutionary processes, error frequency fluctuations in DNA synthesis, stochastic replication patterns of macro molecules ...' – 'Don't give me any more of that nonsense! You're just trying to pull my leg! I don't understand a word.' – 'Well, anyway, Schack is one of our best people. Always just missing the Nobel Prize. As you may know, it's not always the best people who get it, ha ha ... What's that you're saying? Schack with the boss? Can't imagine it. No, he's got nothing at all to do with nuclear power. Interesting. Please keep me informed.'

Instead I was kept informed. I won't forget that excursion so quickly. Unpleasant drizzle all the way up the Ahr valley, then we stopped, in the middle of nowhere. Two hours walk over the stubble and through the mud, and at only six degrees. The conversation was absurd. I had to listen to it all, because we went in one car, which actually should never happen at security level 1. The boss was as trusting as a child, practically eating out of the man's hand. I couldn't believe my ears. By the time we had passed Lengsdorf I had learned that he wanted to know the following: why any at all worthwhile goal is unattainable in politics, and why it transforms itself beyond recognition as soon as one gets close to it. – 'But what do you mean, Mr Chancellor? Your successes ...' – 'Successes, nonsense. I know that's what people say, but between the two of us ...' What people liked to call successes, had never been what was intended, but something else, a third thing, that he had never really thought of. Pause.

Schack, not in the least put out by these quite childish confessions, stops in the middle of the field – by this time we were wading through the German spring – looks through his coat pockets and very calmly lights a cigar. I can see it coming: he's going to make a long digression. My slip-ons are already completely soaked through, and the security men, keeping fifty metres distance, are slapping their padded jackets with impatience and cold.

Schack, small and fat, his hat tipped back on his head, doesn't really look like a research scientist at all, but more like an old-fashioned New York estate agent. 'Systematic causes,' he says loudly. 'Uncontrollable turbulence appears in every sufficiently extensive system, and it does so independently of the behaviour of individual elements. It's simply a question of complexity. It increases discontinuously with a growing metabolism or energy and information flows. Do you follow me? Good. From this perspective we can distinguish between subcritical, critical and hypercritical systems; and you Mr Chancellor, simply have to operate in a hypercritical system, that's all.'

I'm repeating his jargon as best as I can. 'But that's only the beginning,' he continued. 'As long as you haven't grasped the characteristics of hypercritical systems,' – Schack was in full flow now and gesticulating like some Montenegrin – 'you naturally blame the most obvious disturbance variable for the turbulence that appears, i.e. in your case first and foremost you blame your opponents. You look for scapegoats, idiots, saboteurs, try to expand control mechanisms, to eliminate troublemakers, no matter what the issue is, the Atlantic Alliance, the financing of pensions, employment programmes. Result: even more confusion. From that you then draw the conclusion that the measures weren't thoroughgoing enough, and you redouble your efforts.'

Exactly! The boss nods, feels someone understands him. Grim satisfaction. 'But you misjudge the situation! You behave as if the world, i.e. in this case German society, the community, including the armaments lottery, the pensions mess and so on, in short, the system, *had not yet developed far enough*. Something or other is missing: the right theory, the fine tuning, the planning data. As if the whole thing was not yet sufficiently rational, not sufficiently evolved. A typical mistake! A typical failure to recognize the structural characteristics of hypercomplex systems!'

At this point I lost my patience, and I asked him what hypercomplex was supposed to mean, it was all Greek to me. He gave me a contemptuous look.

'As A.N. Kolmogorov demonstrated as long ago as 1965, a system is hypercomplex when, and only when, the information content of the algorithm required to describe it, is approximately equal to the information content of the whole system.' And with that he had shut me up.

'But to come back to your problematic, Mr Chancellor: these development models with their stereotyped optimism have established themselves in the natural sciences, too, for over a hundred years. First of all some kind of principle has to be established, some condition attained: industrialization, basic research, victory in the class struggle, democracy, abolition of poverty, birth control, the welfare state – only then, when that has been achieved, will there be clarity, will planning be possible, will disturbance variables disappear, or they will be so reduced in scale that they can be ignored. Result: a governable world. That would be fine of course, for you at least. . .

'But unfortunately we've learned – I'm simplifying of course – that the higher a system's level of development, the less the condition of the system can be controlled. Examples: central nervous system, planned economy, Gödel's theorem in mathematics, popular democratic parties in domestic politics, parking places in the cities. It's the same everywhere.'

At the mention of 'popular democratic parties' a sigh from the boss. Clearly I had underestimated Schack; the man had a very good idea of where he wanted to get to.

'Parking places?' I asked. 'Why parking places?'

'A very good question,' replied the professor. Conceited little nonentity, I thought, but didn't, however, let myself be provoked.

'Using the parking place syndrome I shall demonstrate the conclusion which is perhaps the most important one for you. With all hypercomplex systems the question of what keeps them alive arises – alive, of course, in a metaphoric sense – i.e. what actually prevents them from collapsing.'

'That's a question I've sometimes asked myself too,' muttered the old man.

'Well, the answer is simple. It is just those very disturbances which irritate you, gentlemen, and which you'd so very much like to eliminate.'

'Does that mean, without Eppler no SPD?'

'I can't pass judgement on that. But, if you'll allow me, let's stay with parking places for a moment. The traffic system of a large city is a clear example of hypercomplexity. I think we're agreed on that. All criteria are satisfied: the preponderance of pure stochastic processes, the enormous metabolism, the considerable interdependence, the impossibility of predicting on the basis of any number of known past situations $n$, a future situation $n+1$. Now, an attempt is made to bring this non-deterministic system under control by laws, traffic signs, the police, sanctions, and to achieve perfect regulation by use of traffic lights, television cameras, computers. I don't need to tell you what the result looks like.'

'Nevertheless,' I said, 'the whole things still keeps moving.'

'Yes, but why? Because the participants, the drivers, don't stick to the rules. The strict observance of the traffic regulations would be the end of traffic. In West German cities 55–60 per cent of all parking and stopping practices are illegal. The rule can only be upheld at the cost of its continual infringement. Anarchy prevents chaos. And if that's the case with driving a car, then I can easily imagine what things look like in politics. No, Mr Chancellor, you are really not to be envied.'

We had arrived in a bleak little hole. On the road sign I saw that it was called Dümpelfeld, a name that speaks for itself. The security men had guided the car up by radio, obviously in the hope that our marathon would come to an end sometime. It was already half dark as we climbed in. It was pleasantly warm in the car. I pulled off my dirt-caked shoes without the boss noticing. His face in the rear-view mirror had taken on a thoughtful expression.

'But if one thinks what you're saying, through to the end ...'

'Yes?'

'That would then mean that it's the tax dodgers, the expense account fiddlers and all the rest, who are saving the state from bankruptcy.'

'One could put it that way. Yes.'

'Refusing to obey orders, drunkenness, absence without leave, would be so many guarantees that the Federal army is functioning properly.'

'Quite right.'

'Absenteeism, working in the shadow economy, fraud, smuggling, corruption ...'

'Certainly. Only let me point out that your depiction of this state of affairs is rather one-sided. The list could easily be supplemented by ways of behaving to which even you could not object.'

'For example.'

'For example, "improvisation", "market", "private initiative", "flexibility". Think of the civil servant who in an urgent matter short-circuits the official channels, or of the small businessman who finds a gap, a niche, or the silent sabotage of nonsensical rules and instructions. All very positive, you must admit. In my institute, which is certainly not a large enterprise, we *have to* deceive the ministry, the research council, or let's say, rather, make small corrections to our budget – where would we be otherwise! In practice breaking the rules is an absolute necessity. And it's exactly the same with theory. You won't get far with mere deduction, with 'derivations' from some kind of established natural law. What's crucial, as Kuhn already showed in 1962, are the repairs, the patching up, the cribs, the paradigm shifts. After all, science, too, is a hypercomplex system which both brings forth and requires a welter of countersystemic subsystems.

'After all, it's not just by chance that these subsystems not only survive, but flourish magnificently. Just think of Italy, a country that has been bankrupt for twenty years, and yet it's irrepressible, a riddle for the experts. The solution, if one can call it a solution, is *economia sommersa*, the submerged economy. That's what Italians call whole sectors of production and social life which have escaped interference from the political parties, trade union sclerosis, the inland revenue bureaucracy. Simply dived out of sight, inaccessible and enormously productive. This invisible hand is also capable of criminal impulses, admittedly. But in a way, what we call crime, is anyway only a corrective ... Of course, I don't mean that in a moral sense, but in terms of how systems work...

'Or look at Hungary, which owes its little bit of future to the famous remnants of the past. The state sector is stagnating, it's the most joyless form of extravagance. Fulfilment of the plan and economic death are very close to one another. It's the 'tolerated marginal phenomena' which set labour power and innovation free. Of course, those in charge only realized that when they had no other choice left, but still ... The shadow economy, the grey and black markets have won all along the line. You can also see from this example that hypercomplex systems establish their specific characteristics quite independently of "blocs", "camps", ideological trivia ... Please don't look at me with such dismay. It's not my fault either...

'You see, in such a system there simply isn't any planning, any strategy, any programme that would be intelligent enough to avoid catastrophes, still less to make further evolution possible. The more universal the claims made for proposed solutions, the more useless they are. The more comprehensive and centralist the control is, the more unstable the whole thing becomes. That's particularly evident from attempts at violent solutions. Of course, you can respond with repression and terror, as in Poland or San Salvador, but you only achieve the opposite of what was intended. That also explains the helplessness of the superpowers. A few hundred adolescents in Iran trample the prestige of the United States under foot, or Mr Sadat kicks out the Soviets over-night. And it's for these very same reasons that you have so many problems with so-called major projects: Brokdorf, Gorleben, Startbahn West,* the Rhine–Main–Danube Canal. The more pig-headedly, if you'll excuse the term, such decisions are stuck to, the sooner the decision-makers are at their wits' end as to how to proceed. Today you must expect every important piece of legislation to have effects which will take you by surprise ... Ungovernability ... Yes, one can call it that too, of course. But what does that mean after all?'

---

*Respectively, a nuclear power plant, a nuclear waste-disposal plant – which was never completed – and a new runway at Frankfurt Airport. [Tr.]

We had been on the motorway for some time. The professor shut up at last. It began to rain again. The boss muttered quietly to himself: 'Dreadful ... that would be dreadful.'

In order not to fall asleep, I resolved on frontal attack.

'I ask myself whether what you're preaching there, Professor Schack, doesn't overstep the limits of your discipline? That may be all very well in theoretical biology. I've nothing against Darwin or your amino acids – but politically, if you'll excuse me, such ideas lead to a dead end. That's really all we needed, to have corruption and white-collar crime legitimated by academics. Such old-fashioned qualities as a sense of responsibility, doing one's duty and solidarity are evidently not compatible with your hypercomplex systems, to say nothing at all of sensible planning, long-term thinking and theoretically grounded action in the interests of society as a whole. Instead you preach short-sightedness, *catch as catch can*, in short the survival of the fittest. Or not?'

'Your subordinate is really getting his teeth into it,' remarked the professor and glanced at the boss with a twinkle in his eyes.

'Point one. I have never claimed that I'm particularly competent in ideological questions. We're having a quite informal conversation here, at the invitation of the Federal Chancellor. Your objection is severely critical, but I don't quite know what it's directed against. Either you're denying that we're dealing with a hypercomplex social system – you would, however, have difficulty proving the contrary – or you're maintaining that such a system would be conceivable without deviationists, heretics, doubters, dissidents, renegades. It's unclear to me how you want to justify such a position.

'Point two. It's always the central authorities who try to turn objective problems into moral issues. Because who defines "responsible behaviour", party discipline, the common good, national interests? Evidently you feel called upon to make such judgements. The national good is whatever suits your book and doesn't inconvenience the government.'

I made my reply as polite as possible.

'You overestimate my ambition and my powers, Mr Schack.' He continued as if he hadn't heard me.

'And if that doesn't work, if you lose control, then it's anarchy, the end of the world and so on.

'Point three. I'm far from wanting to justify anything and even less do I want to preach. That's not my job as a scientist. I'm only confirming what happens to be the case.'

At last we turned into Reuterstrasse. The prospect of at last seeing the back of this pig-headed chatterer almost made me cheerful. The boss dismissed me somewhat absent-mindedly.

In the evening, draft of the Bremen speech, coalition discussion paper, submissions for Brussels, reply to B. Went to bed dead tired.

*Friday.* Exceptionally, a completely smooth day, everything routine. However, the boss's condition gives me cause for worry. He's not bellowing today, he appears lost in thought, which I personally find worse.

Ambassador G. asks me after lunch: 'What's up with him? I had the feeling the whole time he wasn't really paying any attention.'

In the afternoon he signs everything that's put in front of him without comment. Not a good omen.

*Saturday.* Peace at last. 2 × 5mg. Valium. At Lily's in the afternoon.

*Sunday.* Still early morning when the phone rings. L. at the other end of the line. Was with the boss last night, quite informally, at home, for a couple of beers. 'Aha. And you wake me up at this unearthly hour, just to tell me the happy news?' But the evening had been odd somehow, the boss had displayed a cheerfulness which had been a bit strange. Constantly insisting how much he was looking forward to the summer: then he could go sailing again at last, for weeks on end. It sounds suspiciously like he's thinking of resigning. I reassure him. Nothing out of the ordinary is happening, there's nothing new about his mood, and it's hardly surprising given this pigsty. Those were the usual threats which not a soul took seriously any more.

Hardly has he put the phone down when there's another call. This time it's the Minister. The boss is saying things which don't make any sense. *He* has requested a statement on the steel issue, and because of last night's Washington statement, the press already scented blood, but the Chancellor hadn't responded at all, had waffled on about spontaneous, uncontrollable oscillations, about entropy, Gödel theorems, as if he was repeating a school textbook; could I explain it. Then the penny dropped.

'I know where he's got it from,' I said. 'That was all we needed. It's gale force nine, and what's the captain doing? Instead of sending all men to the pumps, he decides to become a biologist, to go back to university and study systems theory or thermodynamics, or God knows what. Right, I propose we meet at the office in half an hour, informally of course, on no account must the press get wind of anything. And something else. If at all possible, can I ask you to bring in State Secretary K. from the Research Ministry, and someone from the party executive committee too, of course.'

He was somewhat surprised, but I was able to convince him that it was high time to do something. I dressed myself cursing. Glorious weather outside, people out for a drive. At the Meckenheimer Strasse lights an idiot who can't brake drives into my back; fortunately he only smashed the left tail light.

When all the gentlemen had at last arrived – K. had to be fetched from the golf course – it was quarter to twelve. There was a mood of puzzlement, everyone was trying to guess what was up. I gave a brief but precise summary of the conversations during that horrible stroll.

'I don't understand why he's taken it all so much to heart. It's all pure theory!' said L.

'I do,' declared the representative from the party executive. 'All I need to say is "Popper". Do you remember the time he discovered Popper? We had to listen to it for three months. "The Poverty of Historicism." "The Open Society and its Enemies." And that wasn't all! I remember very well how he tormented the whole Cabinet with the indeterminacy theorem. And in the middle of one of our party executive sessions when we were discussing personnel questions, he suddenly claimed that Wehner's objection was nonsense because not falsifiable. Wehner was so astonished that his pipe went out.'

'Well gentlemen,' said the Minister, 'what do you propose?'

There was a lengthy pause.

'Schack,' I said eventually, 'put all this stuff into his head. Schack will have to talk it all out again.'

'Why don't we have him flown in, by helicopter? Today even.'

'And then what?'

'He must just simply and calmly ring the bungalow doorbell.'

'But not before we've hauled him over the coals.'

'And what if he doesn't want to?'

'Just let me deal with it,' I said. 'He'll come round all right. I know my man.'

After tea, just before six, the boss was in a cheerful mood. I took Schack to the landing strip.

'I would like to thank you sincerely,' I said reluctantly, 'on behalf of all of us, for finding the time. . .'

'On the contrary,' he exclaimed, 'I have to thank you for giving me the opportunity to clear up a misunderstanding that would have been quite fatal to me. . .'

'How did it go then?'

'As predicted. The minister briefed me thoroughly after all. What he told me was completely right. The Chancellor had drawn quite extreme, and I must say altogether false, conclusions from our conversation in the Ahr valley. That's just the kind of risk there is when one – if you'll forgive me – confronts a complete layman with a scientific theory. The layman tends always to hear only what he *wants* to hear.'

'In this case that he might just as well withdraw to his sailing boat. . .'

'A depressing thought! Of course the exact opposite is true.'

'You'll have to explain that to me. Because after everything you came up with recently, a conclusion like that seems the obvious one.'

'Quite simple. Of course the Chancellor can never "win". And you know the reasons for that. But that's a long way from saying that he's not needed or even that he's superfluous. On the contrary! On the contrary!'

'Why on the contrary?'

'Well, I ask you! After all is said and done a hypercomplex system is still a system and not a refuse dump. That means it necessarily collapses as soon as you remove the elements that structure it, even if those elements can never ever prevail completely. In order to avoid the term *dialectic*, which I don't like to use – it's rather discredited scientifically – we can employ other expressions. Think, for example, of Gödel's statements on axiomatic theory. You know, Gödel's 1931 theorem.'

'No, I don't know. Every time you start lecturing, you pull this Gödel out of your hat. The name means nothing to me. I'm not an encyclopedia. You wouldn't like it very much either if I was constantly coming at you with swap arrangements and harmonization figures.'

'I'm really sorry.'

'Then explain to me in simple words what you're trying to say with this jack-in-the-box called Gödel.'

'Very simple. Every mathematical structure relies on a series of basic assumptions or axioms. The axioms that are chosen must not contradict one another. The rest is system-building according to the laws of formal logic. Now if you develop a system beyond a relatively simple stage you reach a point at which it is no longer possible to demonstrate the absence of contradiction in the system with the means available to it.'

'Ah. So that's what it's like in mathematics.'

'And so, if even in mathematics, in the field of pure theory, no absence of contradiction is possible, what on earth will things be like in biological or social systems.'

'Quite a bold analogy. I don't know what your Mr Gödel would think about it.'

'Gödel's neither here nor there,' exclaimed the professor – he was talking more loudly, because the pilot began to run the engine when he saw us coming. 'At any rate the central instances in complex systems never get what they want. In fact without the disturbance variables they would be destroyed. But one can and must turn this argument around. Without popular democratic parties no Greens, without the Seven Sisters no independent petrol stations, without policemen no robbers, without law and order no anarchy ... Which should demonstrate your boss's indispensability clearly enough.'

I laughed. 'My dear professor, all that theory, and that's what comes out of it in the end? The hypercomplex mountain of Göttingen labours, and what does it give birth to? A theoretical mouse!'

'What do you expect?' he said, shrugging his shoulders. 'Even basic research is not so different from anything else ... Apart from that, the mouse is one of evolution's most successful products and is likely to outlive every prophet.'

Suddenly, despite all his nonsense, his cigar and his false bonhomie, he seemed quite likeable. I called after him, as he was climbing into the helicopter: 'First you tear open a hole, then you fill it up again.'

'At least that way,' he shouted, 'we're not going to be out of a job.'

I didn't get home until just before midnight. The pavements were blocked for miles with waiting cars. The Nigerian embassy was evidently holding a huge garden party. Presumably it was the unavoidable national holiday. All that mattered now was not to bump into any acquaintance. The crisis, if it was a crisis at all and not a false alarm, was averted. But one never knows. Postponement, winning time, is everything in our business. I left my car in the middle of the no-parking zone.

(*1982*)

# 6

# Blind-Man's-Buff Economics

The serious German daily newspaper breaks down into a number of parts, just as the German infantry rifle once did. The practised reader knows what must be done to strip it down in a matter of seconds. He removes supplements for the toddler and for the mountain climber and all the other advertising plantations, by plucking them out of the loose bundle and throwing them away. The financial and business pages usually fall victim to a similar reflex action.* It's a pity, because these pages, easily recognizable from the endless columns of figures, have deserved a better fate.

I wouldn't dare to claim that they make exciting reading. I must also admit that the prose of the company and Stock Exchange reports is perhaps even clumsier than that of the home news section. Yet, for all that, a luxuriant language runs riot on this barren soil. An engineering company sees 'a hint of silver on the horizon'; the champagne trade is 'not bubbling over with joy'; 'Coloroll shares take a pasting'; 'Marmite spreads over to the US'; and so on and so on. The modest humour of such

---

*What in Britain are called the financial or business pages, in German-speaking countries go under the heading of economy or economics section. In the original German version of the essay, therefore, the reference to economy and economics is much more direct than is usual in English. I have used the words 'business', 'finance', and 'economics' depending on which I thought was most appropriate in context, but the German usage should be borne in mind. [Tr.]

phrases corresponds to the solemn inflection and the delightful naivety of the financial section. Here honest happiness at higher dividends and genuine sorrow over an all too rare 'fall in prices' are still the rule. Anyone making a profit is good, while the Internal Revenue Department and the trade unions are bad. Here everything's still right with the world, and so consequently anyone who offends 'business' is given tight-lipped warnings, subjected to old-maidish reproof, and venomously abused only in the most extreme emergency; on the other hand there are virtually never any outright lies like those in the political commentaries and the leading articles. Lies could have fatal consequences where business decisions are concerned, that is, where cash is at stake. Once one has become more familiar with the surroundings the pleasant feeling grows that here one is among friends, shielded from a troublesome outside world by a special language evocative of the padded leather doors of a boring but well-run club in which one can continue to rely on the professional zeal of the staff, which in this case means the journalists.

I have often asked myself who or what 'the economy' really is. To judge by the family record that I unfold every morning over breakfast, it can only consist of a tiny minority. I have come to the conclusion that 'the economy' consists principally of 'business leaders'; that these leaders deal with seven- to eleven-digit sums, and are correspondingly oppressed by their responsibilities, and that their lives are practically identical with 'economic life'. In addition, these 'business leaders' have their associations and federations which are also part of the economy. When the representatives of these organizations are forced to travel by plane, and usually on the so-called business shuttle, they read the financial pages.

Although I try to keep up with my reading of them, I can't get rid of the feeling that, as a reader, I'm out of place. The commentator is pleased because the New Zealand loan has been taken up so well. On the other hand, Paris was listless at the close of trading, gold mines lost some ground, and liquidations were noted among professional traders. Hapag–Lloyd, we have learned, wants to raise earnings, and Mannesmann's profits have increased again. It all goes on, day in, day out, behind my back as it were. I must admit that I don't belong to 'the economy'. If at least I were an 'ordinary saver', or a 'small shareholder'! Because these characters are welcomed with open arms, and the editors' concern for them is moving, as if they were dealing with the walking wounded, even if an undertone of condescension is also unmistakable. These people belong, but only as onlookers. I, by contrast, only participate in 'economic life', if at all, in a quite subordinate way, as an 'employee' for example, or as a 'consumer'; in a word as an object of the 'economy', i.e. as its fool.

Well, one doesn't have to belong to everything, I say to myself, grit my teeth and read on. It is often amusing and always instructive to listen to the speeches of people who consider themselves to be insiders. I've often immersed myself in trade magazines like 'The German Shepherd Dog' or 'The Central Wood Association News' for that very reason, and I've never been disappointed! The involuntary is their strength, and I forgive them everything for they know not what they say. The most important message of the business and financial sections, and one which they repeat daily, without realizing it, is this: democracy must not stick its nose in wherever money is at stake.

For example, a business journalist will always describe a car factory as if it was his own private property. From this perspective, the fact that other people besides the major shareholders are involved in the operation of such an enterprise, a few tens of thousands of shop-floor and office workers, for example, appears as an unfortunate by-product; at most these persons are responsible for unreasonably high wage costs. The reporter isn't at all interested in the firm's product either; and the hundred thousand people for whom it is produced lead only a shadowy existence under the heading 'falling home demand'.

In the financial pages the majority is only of importance at the annual general meeting, and there care is taken to ensure that it stays where it belongs, that is, in the hands of the minority. The financial editor doesn't woo readers. On the contrary, if they've got nothing to invest he chases them away. That's why the financial press is agreeably free of demagoguery and why *Bild* newspaper has to do without a business section. In his stubborn innocence, the journalist who casts a glance at business and the economy every morning expresses what his colleagues in the other sections successfully deny: that he is his master's voice, and that a newspaper doesn't exist to represent the interests of its readers but those of its owners.

The question, who or what 'the economy' is can therefore be answered quite easily. 'The economy' is nothing more than an affectionate nickname for capital. It's not news to me that the press feels a need to rename everything and I'm prepared to put up with this linguistic prescription if I have to. I have greater difficulty with my next question. It goes: Does the economy, does business, know what it's doing?

As far as I can see there is only one place in which this enquiry is answered with a resounding yes: in the advertisement section which follows the business and economic pages much as the pickpocket follows his victim. 'Investments – Transactions – Capital Movement': whereas the editorial pages display caution, reserve, discretion and hold out the prospect of a final judgement only for the distant future, when it's a question of what to do with the ready millions, then carefree certainty beams from every advertisement.

Here the message is grab before it's too late, get on the train before it leaves. Exceptionally high, bank-secured yields beckon, exceptional tax advantages, absolutely safe, no-risk investment strategies. The consultants at work here seem to have aimed at robbing me of my least doubt that business knows 100 per cent what it's doing. I don't wish to offend any of these gentlemen but I must confess that their promises strike me as a feeble copy of that unrivalled, unrepeatable advert that proclaims: send me 5 dollars in an envelope and I will tell you how to increase your capital 100 times over in less than a month! The answer which arrives by printed paper rate, is, of course: do exactly what I'm doing.

Now, of course, conmen who try to draw money out of our pockets with nonsensical promises are not usually considered to be business leaders, nor are business leaders thought of as being conmen. Yet this distinction is only reassuring at first sight. While the 'black sheep' which, as we all know are to be found everywhere and therefore also in the advertisement pages of newspapers sensitive about their reputation, swear black and blue that they're infallible when it comes to turning your modest savings into millions, the really serious top manager can be recognized by his inability to guarantee anything. He's tapping in the dark; he muddles through; he has more bad luck or perhaps even good luck than judgement; in short, he's a person like you or I, the only difference is that he's at the top of a large company. This is what one has to try and imagine: the whole show stumbling along in the fog behind the top man, as if it's follow-my-leader, with countless dangers lurking all around. And he's always right at the front like some poor minesweeper. One wrong step and everything goes up. It's a job for tough, lonely, courageous men; because when yet again something goes wrong who stands by the man at the top? No one! He has to take his hat and retire to his estates – that's how ungrateful the world is.

Then a new but tried and tested man has to jump into the breach. Fresh blood or old hand, or both at the same time, someone or other will be found who can reorganize, restructure, consolidate and restore the shop's financial soundness, whether it's called Chrysler, Leyland or AEG. A few hundred million here or there don't matter in such cases which, after all, are of national importance. And if all the ropes break then there's still one person left to turn to – the Minister of Finance. When the failure has reached really monumental dimensions, he pays. Does business know what it's doing? As I said, I don't belong, I'm speaking as a complete outsider, I can only pass on my impressions, and they come to this: business doesn't have a clue.

In order to be sure of this point I very much wanted to question its representatives, the representatives of business themselves. I thought for a long time about how I might go about this. A completely relaxed conversation, in familiar surroundings, in the middle of the manager's everyday working life would be best, I decided. I resolved to spend a morning in the lift of the head office of a large Frankfurt bank. Each time a business leader appeared, I politely asked him whether, in his opinion, business knew what it was doing. Due to their brevity, conversations in a lift produce concise formulations. Here I can only pass on three of the most valuable answers: 1. 'If you always knew in advance which number you were going to draw, the whole game would lose its appeal.' 2. 'Business doesn't know what it's doing, and there, young man, is just where the famous entrepreneurial risk comes in.' 3. 'After all, even the best gambler can't win every time.'

I understand all that. But actually I wasn't looking for a sure-fire tip; and so while the lift's electronic *ping!* sounded and red numbers flickered into life and disappeared, I objected diffidently that I was less bothered about boom or slump, cash or bills, than – excuse me! – about the thing as a whole: how it all works, whether it's possible to make sense of the rules of the game, in other words, whether business sees 'the economy' as an intelligible process, or merely a blind fumbling in the dark.

Ah, said my informants, as if with one voice, we're not responsible for that, the thing as a *whole* isn't our problem, after all, we've got our own show to take care of. The whole, they said, is a question of the general framework, of key data, of the influence of foreign trade movements, of commodity prices, of the long-term outlook for energy supply; there's economic policy, budgetary policy, social policy, trade-cycle management policy, public order policy, fiscal policy, foreign policy, demographic policy, money-supply policy questions. In such matters people like us, they said in conclusion, finger on the button which stops the chrome doors snapping shut before they step out of the lift, can only make representations, register doubts, in a word: pray, but nobody listens to us at all, the politicians just settle it all between themselves, you should take up questions like that with the political parties and the state.

The state! So it's the state that's supposed to understand, see things as a whole, know what's going on – just when the old hands, the bankers and the industrialists throw in the towel and assure the world of their impotence! Now, one doesn't need to tug at the state's sleeves between one floor and the next, as with the gentlemen from the board of directors. No, the state always has time for us. The state makes its pronouncements on television every evening. The Chancellor of the Exchequer gives an interview, the President of the Republic makes a speech, the Minister of Finance mutters on a talk show, the Party Chairman holds his own at a press conference. And whatever words these gentlemen use, irrespective of whether they're Social Democrats or Frenchmen or lumps of vomit or Liberals or monetarists or Danes, the message that comes out in the end is always the same: the state rubs its eyes when it looks at the economy, it's astonished when it opens the newspaper and discovers yet again that something completely unforeseen has happened. Whether it's about certain sureties in the construction industry which, quite suddenly, are due to be paid or of credits to Poland worth billions which are overdue; whether yawning gaps have suddenly appeared in the pension insurance fund; whether the German electronics industry is finished, or the Federal Railways 'can't be financed any more' – the poor old state learns about all these things over breakfast, just like you or I. The state is a complete layman just like you or I. After each blow, the state staggers on with a vacant expression from one deficit to the next, like a punchdrunk boxer. Sometimes it's possible to feel really sorry for this booby who, every time a multipurpose combat plane is needed or a surface-to-surface missile, lets himself be taken for a sucker by some carpet salesman or other. Evidently the state can't do its sums. That's the only explanation for the disappearance of thousands of millions from the till overnight, and the fact that the budget has holes in it, like a pair of tights from the end of summer sales, even before it's been passed by Parliament.

Not that I would want to place the Federal government in a false light with my remarks! The state is an economic cretin, and that holds true regardless of who happens to be in power at any time, of what the government thinks, and what it would like to make us believe. The President of the United States, for example, although he is far from being a Social Democrat, is just as much a master of idle and futile arithmetic as the Cabinet in Bonn. Years ago, he promised everyone who wanted to hear that he would lower taxes, but also double and triple arms expenditure. In the opinion of Dr Reagan this is an infallible method for fighting inflation and reviving the American economy. Any schoolchild could have proved the opposite, even without a pocket calculator; but who wants to ask the advice of a school-child when the economic policy of a superpower is at stake? For that only the best is good enough and the best of the best is Dr Stockman.

'None of us really understands what's happening with all these figures,' says David A. Stockman, the American president's budget director and his chief adviser on all financial, tax and budget questions. 'The assumptions on which our budget is based were completely arbitrary.'

I've always suspected it, of course. But is that a comfort? That business doesn't know what it's doing; that it earns money just as instinctively as a hen cackles or a mosquito bites, even going bankrupt if necessary, seems strange enough to me; but I find it alarming that the governments of the most important countries in the world should organize their economic policies on the principle of blind-man's-buff.

Only, in such a situation, to whom can one turn with a plea for further information? I was unsure. A fortunate accident came to my aid. At a reception to mark the umpteenth recurrence of the day on which Prussia became a kingdom or Goethe died or some insurance company was founded, a youthful-looking gentleman dressed in light blue who was making a careful analysis of the buffet was pointed out to me. He was the economic affairs spokesman of one of the few parties which in this country share out the buffet among themselves. I hastened to confide my doubts to him.

'You can't be serious,' said the spokesman, a lobster between his lips. 'The state certainly can't concern itself with such questions. The state doesn't think, it acts. I know what you're going to ask me!' – he stretched out his free hand towards me defensively, picking up a canapé with the other: 'How? You're going to ask me, how does the state act, according to which criteria, and with what justification? Just between the two of us, it muddles through. But, of course, it's preferable to give the outside world an impression of authority, to appear competent. Now, for that purpose we have experts. We don't think, we let others do the thinking for us! After all, we don't just have business and the economy, there's also economics. I studied political economy for years, I know what I'm talking about. Unbelievable confusion! Inflation and deflation, micro and macro, upswing and downswing. I know what you want to ask me: Does economics know what it knows? The answer to that question must unfortunately be: it's all bluff. Please don't quote me. But in this field you can become famous with the most utter nonsense. Have you heard of Laffer, Arthur B. Laffer? Highly paid man in the USA, influential, fashionable – supply side economics, you get the picture! Now, Professor Laffer is the inventor of the Laffer Curve, which is named after Professor Laffer. An indispensable aid for drawing up a modern taxation policy. It shows you how tax yield can be maximized. If, for example, you impose zero per cent taxes on income, consumption and profits, then your tax revenue equals zero. Do you follow me? Good. Now, if you raise the percentage level of taxation, the Laffer curve rises and you collect more taxes. Great idea, you'll say. But be careful! Assuming you keep on raising the level of taxation, you impose taxes of 70, 80, 90, 95 per cent – what happens then? People lose interest, they stop working, shopping, making profits, and when taxation reaches 100 per cent, where does the Laffer Curve end up? You've guessed it, at zero! Who would have thought it. Now you'll say, what's so clever about that, only Dr Reagan could fall for a conman like that, it's not serious economics, it's charlatanry! But that just shows you don't know anything about economists. Because they've always had a taste for curves of one kind or another.

'Do you know what a Kitchin is? A Kitchin is a period of approximately three-and-a-half years. A Juglar, on the other hand, lasts seven to ten years, while a Kondratiev, if I'm not mistaken, spreads over fifty to sixty years. In other words, one Kondratiev ▬ 5–8 Juglars ▬ 14–17 Kitchins. That's what the trade-cycle researchers, after whom these periods of time are named, have come up with, in effect long, medium and short cycles. Up and down, sometimes faster, sometimes slower. You won't believe it, but at university I had to learn this nonsense off by heart. It's true that Nikolai D. Kondratiev has gone a little out of fashion since then, but no need to worry, after all, now we have Professor Friedman and Professor Laffer, and in the Federal Republic – please don't quote me – we have the four or five wise men, that is, the committee of experts. We also have the annual reports of the economic research institutes, we have institutes of trade-cycle research, for the world economy, for research into business concentration, for research into the conditions for producing reports on overall economic development, etc., etc.

'But, if you ask me – do you know Eliot? "Between the idea and the reality,/Between the motion and the act,/Falls the shadow!" In other words: don't let them make you believe that it's your fault, that it's all Greek to you as soon as these gentlemen start talking about market stimuli, money supply goals and investment blockages. The margin of error of their highly paid prognoses is around 40–50 per cent. It's a scatter-shot principle, no different from the infallible system for roulette that someone might try to sell you.'

He was silent for a moment while he tried the venison pâté, but he didn't take his eyes off me. He always knew in advance what I was going to ask him, so it was really quite unnecessary to speak in the presence of the spokesman. 'Don't imagine,' he continued, 'that I particularly dislike economists! Quite the opposite, I find their tricks much more entertaining than the press statements I have to draw up every day. Apart from that, there are enough other branches of scholarship that come up with incredible results. Just think of the astrophysicists and their black holes, the sociologists and their interaction models, the neo-structuralists with their desiring machines – they're all nothing more than tellers of tales, alchemists, fortune-tellers, who might as well be reading coffee-grounds!

'The economists' reports are just the same. At worst they serve as a loin cloth for naked interest; as a somewhat faded fig leaf in the struggle between employers and unions – but even that would perhaps be taking them all too seriously. No, no, the reader of the *Financial Times* shouldn't be deprived of what the reader of *Bild* gets. Everybody has a right to a daily horoscope. Fortune-tellers never lose, they're irrefutable because disproving their prognoses doesn't hurt them, it only increases the need for new prognoses. But you look quite depressed! You mustn't take it all so seriously!'

The economics spokesman, a cheerful man, dressed completely in light blue, tried to comfort me.

'But the economy,' I objected, 'controls our fate!'

'Exactly,' he said, swallowed a piece of real Cheddar cheese, and like a little general cast a satisfied glance over the ravaged buffet.

(*1982*)

# 7

## A Plea for the Home Tutor:

## A Little Bit of Educational Policy

I never liked going to school, neither did Joseph, never mind Edith. Tucker always played truant. Albert Kuchen, nicknamed Dog-biscuit [*Hundekuchen*], didn't want to, Gertrude failed her school leaving certificate, Roly Grütz repeated twice, Milly Guggemoos hated every single one of the teachers. Only Rainer felt at ease at grammar school, but he was always a swot anyway; and as for Rümmelein, well, for Rümmelein school was a kind of refuge because he was beaten at home, and in the schoolyard he at least got something to eat; apart from that the school was heated.

At the recent high-level discussion between the finance Ministers and the Federal State Commission, the finance Ministers of the individual states firmly insisted that in the key planning year of 1985 only the 85 billion marks approved by them would be available to the educational sector. The talks are said to have been broken off without an agreement being reached. If these planning figures remain unchanged then the present total of approximately 570,000 teaching places will have to be reduced to 520,000 by 1985.

Head of department Vogel is already groaning on Friday evening at the thought of Monday morning. Bernd Bonitz stubbornly insists that the 3,400 marks a month he makes after tax is hard-earned money; the secondary school, he says, is pure hard labour, and he's not going to take it much longer. Miss Zimmerle has got a sick note, her colleague Miss Wildgruber only keeps going with the help of pills. Dr Wartmann is disillusioned,

97

Dr Gross embittered, Mrs von Koegler wants a divorce, and recently at the staff meeting Fritzi Bauriedl said: 'If I hear the words "ratio allocated to the reserve" again I'm going to scream.'

What can be to blame for all this? No one seems to know. Up to now, all the research, no matter how thoroughly it may have been carried out, all reform proposals, all the agreements between Ministers of Culture and Education, all the behavioural studies, all the pilot studies, all the innovation advisory panels, all the compulsory choice differentiation models, all the didactic blueprints, all the evaluation research, all the overall education plans and guidelines have only succeeded in making the long, long, long calamity of school even longer.

I'm almost ashamed to say that I know the answer, that the solution to the problem is quite obvious, that the redeeming word is on the tip of my tongue. I am afraid that it will be taken as a joke or a provocation. Can this complete layman, a writer even, have in his pocket the solution to a puzzle which thousands upon thousands of highly qualified school psychologists, curriculum researchers and educational planners have failed to solve? Well, it's true. I hope the scales will fall from the professionals' eyes and that they will cheerfully clear their desks as soon as the glad tidings reach them.

The commandment by which the state school came into being and by which it still continues to exist today can be seen, resplendent in its innocence, on old schools in the countryside under the faded little picture of Jesus above the gate: 'Suffer the little children to come unto me!' And, however exotic this biblical text may seem to the solid members of the Education and Science Trade Union of today, it just as certainly continues to determine the guiding principles of all state educational policy. Translated into the language of bureaucracy, the old-fashioned motto reads like this: '§ 18, para 1. If a schoolable child does not take part in instruction or in other school events decreed to be compulsory without legitimate cause, then the headmaster can apply to the district authority for the enforcement of attendance. The district authority through its authorized representatives can compel the attendance of the schoolable child at school ...

§ 19, para 1. A fine can be imposed on whoever ... as a school-able child does not take part in instruction or other school events declared to be compulsory.'

That's the General Compulsory Schooling Law in Bavaria; other federal states put it in a similar way; all these laws are based on the National Compulsory Schooling Laws of 1920 and 1938; anyone who wants even more details can read the relevant regulations, which go by such fine names as *ASchO [Allgemeine Schulordnung* – General School Regulations] or *EBASchOG.*

I never enjoyed going to school, but I always enjoyed learning something new. Edith and Tucker did too. With Milly Gugge-moos I'm not so sure. At any rate, I've no time for the fashion-able maxims of Father Illich – 'Education, no thanks!' – and under no circumstances would I wish to advocate Anti-Peda-gogics which, as its name reveals, is only the reverse of pedagogic terror. On the contrary, I would find it altogether agreeable if the population of the Federal Republic, including all the politicians, managers and journalists, was in a position to speak German and even, if possible, to write it. I would like it if children and adults didn't, as usual, go to the dogs; in a word if everyone could do what he is capable of. Yes, I'd like to go even further and state: Our free democratic constitutional order would not even be threatened if there were to be a sudden outbreak of good manners.

I only doubt whether these or any other educational goals can be attained by 'compelling the attendance ... at school' of ourselves or of our children. And I really can't see at all why the mountain should be compelled to come to the prophet when the reverse procedure would be so much more obvious, simple and reasonable. That's why I'm proposing that in the not too distant future the above mentioned 570,000 teachers should get up on their own two feet and seek out their lost sheep. For it's certainly not as though the pupils were there for the teachers. The teachers are there for the pupils. I don't know whether these sentences arouse horror or delight in a teacher's heart. I must, however, express them without regard for such sensitivities, for they constitute the foundation of my proposal. If one weighs them carefully, the conclusion must be that the only true teacher is the home tutor.

Now the home tutor, as we know him from old novels, plays and diaries is an old but by no means respectable figure. I am the first to admit that. A poor devil who sat right at the bottom of the table, he performed his difficult duties for many centuries without the benefit of a pay scheme, without pension rights, without protection against unfair dismissal, to say nothing at all of location and child-number weighting, of job seniority and cost of living allowances. For him the only certainties were everyday humiliation and the ingratitude of his 'patrons'.

With the disappearance of this sad figure, however, there also disappeared the quite obvious principle according to which the unfortunate worked: the children to whom he was supposed to teach something learned in familiar surroundings, within their own four walls, where they were at home – and not in some strange, inhospitable territory, in a ghetto for youth and its tamers, in a hostile building that confronted them as stable, as cage, as prison or as barracks.

The state school has always been the domain of a distant administration, a place of repression devised by neither pupils nor teachers, in which neither have ever had any say. Its buildings were and are architecture of domination. Once they looked like inferior military colleges, today they look like Stammheim high-security prison. A single glance tells one that, like madhouses and reformatories, they have been erected for the custody and disciplining of people. These technocratic dreams cast in concrete are completely unsuitable for learning anything in. The childrens' vandalism, which reveals an admirably energetic resistance, is no more than the determined attempt to get rid of these dangerously unhealthy surroundings. It's remarkably unusual, on the other hand, to hear of children daubing their own home, setting fire to it or smashing it to matchwood. Even in the most crowded council flat the plates usually remain in one piece. The ten-year-olds clearly don't even think of wrecking the refrigerator and throwing the TV set out of the window.

You can't be serious? You want us to show what we can do here at 16 Siegfried Street, fifth floor left, at the Schneidewinds, in an ordinary rented apartment? No need to panic, dear teachers! I still hope to convince you of the excellence of my idea. First of all, no one is suggesting that, like the unhappy Jakob Michael Reinhold Lenz,* you should only be there for the children of the privileged. There's no question of that at the Schneidewinds. Second, you will not as in days gone by be working for charity from the hands of the rich but, just as before, for a reasonable salary out of the tax payer's pocket. And third, you don't need to be afraid that little Helga Schneidewind will be stuck alone in her room day after day just waiting for the teacher to come. You quite rightly argue that it's not a good idea to isolate six or ten year olds from one another, and that children need the company of other children. It's a good thing too; because ten million teachers, one for each child, would be hard to find and even harder to pay. I have learned from a qualified source that the ideal size for 'group interaction' (that's just the curious way in which sociologists express themselves) is five to seven people.

The following experimental arrangement is easily derived from what has been said. At about half past eight in the morning Miss Zimmerle gets into her Volvo yawning quietly and drives to Siegfried Street. On the way she picks up little Falk who lives on a new estate further out of town. Three other children, who live just around the corner, have already gathered at the Schneidewinds.

It's a small three-room apartment. The new shapeless suite has been ordered, but not yet delivered, so the hostess, seven-year-old Helga Schneidewind, has brought a stool from the

---

*German Romantic writer and playwright. he wrote a drama drawing on his experiences as a tutor, and is the subject of the famous story *Lenz* by Büchner. [Tr.]

kitchen. Once the party is complete – five pupils and one teacher – breakfast is quietly eaten. Then work can begin.

Miss Zimmerle no longer needs to spend time on reading and writing, adding and subtracting, these seven-year-olds could do that a long time ago. These are skills which anyone between the ages of four and seventy can acquire in a couple of weeks without any very great effort, unless he happens to go to school; there it can take, depending on circumstances, several years. The absence of supervision by any kind of superior has a beneficial effect on the teaching as does the absence of a timetable. The group chooses its own reading material. Books and teaching materials are paid for out of a small money box Miss Zimmerle always carries in her brief case. The first foreign language can gradually be started in the second or third year. It's astonishing to see how quickly a seven-year-old child is capable of under-standing an American comic. German grammar can be studied using *Bild* newspaper and *Frau im Spiegel* ['Women's Mirror']; first Miss Zimmerle underlines the mistakes in red, then the texts are translated into German collectively and properly edited. But it's also possible to try out the household toys or look at the pictures in Mr Schneidewind's 'Golden Do-It-Yourself Manual'. Since instruction takes place in a different home every day, the need for variety is taken care of. The Stachowiaks, for example, have a balcony, the Krieger family even has a garden with a swimming pool and table tennis. Falk's mother is French, and Mr Falk has recently acquired a video recorder. So now and then a French film is put on; if the plot gets too complicated, Miss Zimmerle provides a commentary. The children like being in a different house every day; one can also call it practical social studies, if you like. When the pupils are hungry, shopping, cooking and washing up are done together.

Sometimes the group gets fed up with always sitting around in flats stuffed full of furniture. Then the children start whispering into Miss Zimmerle's ear: 'We want to go out!' In the place of laboriously planned 'school trips' there is a peripatetic instruction which seeks out its own goal according to weather and mood. There's hardly any semi-public place to which five children can't obtain entrance: radio and TV studio, farm, computer centre, nursery garden, airport, town hall, film studio, car factory, printing works, monastery, luxury hotel. Instead of a fifty-headed horde of shouting, bad-tempered louts, the public would be dealing with five or six quite normal people – a blessing for museum visitors. Perhaps the children will also force their teacher to search out a gym. Their thirst for physical activity is well known to be boundless, and it may be that they long for one of those pedagogic monkey houses which smell of the sweat of fear and where, at a word of command, one can stretch at the high bar and torment oneself on the parallel bars, climb up and down the walls and fiddle about with weights. Or the children demand a couple of hours of competitive sport with stopwatch and whistle. But I doubt it very much; because very few children are masochists, and as for Miss Zimmerle, she doesn't have much time for sadistic drill either. People with reasonably intact emotional drives never ever let the words 'physical exercise' or 'keep fit' cross their lips. That's why the children will shout out at the tops of their voices: 'Let's have a race to Rödelheim Ice Cream Parlour! We're going to build a hut! We're going to play boccia, table tennis, pinball! We're going to the meadows by the river to play football! We're going to fly kites! We're going to build a raft! We're going roller-skating, carting, sledging! We're going to hire a rowing boat! We're organizing a rock'n'roll tournament, an orange-box derby! We're going swimming!' And so on. A pedagogic travelling circus of such tiny dimensions does not require any special organization. It can move around spontaneously and freely. If there's no underground nearby, then if need be Miss Zimmerle's old Volvo can be used.

Learning speed is entirely dependent on the skills and needs of the group. If the teacher is any good – and who could doubt that in the case of Miss Zimmerle? – and if children and parents do their bit, everything goes astonishingly quickly. There's no 'school year', certificates are awarded when the work has been covered. Holidays are taken when it suits everyone. The dates can be worked out with a few telephone calls, and so the much-discussed problem of staggering school holidays is easily disposed of, too. There's no need for *all* the schoolchildren, parents and teachers of Germany to swelter simultaneously in a jam on the Munich–Salzburg autobahn.

The daily working hours of the children and Miss Zimmerle are self-regulating, too. Every household has its own daily routine which can serve as a guide. In total, Miss Zimmerle, ends up with more 'pupil contact hours' than before, of course, but that doesn't mean very much. First of all, she doesn't have to cope with a tribe of thirty to forty howling dervishes, but with five individual people whom she knows very well. Second, she's rid of the staff meetings, the interval supervision, the administrative work, the intrigues and the rows in the staff room. And third, she doesn't have to correct exercise books in the evenings any more, since homework has abolished itself as it were, because all work is done at home. A national tragicomedy with millions of participants has vanished overnight and without a single tear being shed. The blackmail racket of 'extra tutorials' has also disappeared.

School buses and travel passes no longer exist. The journey to school is reduced to a four or five minute walk. Every year a couple of thousand fewer children are killed on the roads. The anonymity of the school is over and done with. Everyone concerned, including the parents, knows exactly whom they're dealing with. Problems are identified in good time. If there's a row, the child or the teacher can change groups. The word *class* already sounds quite anachronistic. The group isn't formed because of a call-up order, but rather through co-optation.

Crowds of bureaucrats who were busy getting in the way of pupils and teachers with regulations, syllabuses, standardization manuals, survey forms, guidelines and examination rules, can be sent home or given useful work. The home-tutor system makes the state surveillance apparatus largely superfluous. The need for institutional supervision is really just as irrational as the fear of anarchy. The capacity of small-scale social situations to regulate themselves can be observed in the arrival lounge of any airport. As one's own suitcase, a sacrosanct object, the very embodiment of private property, glides majestically in on the conveyor belt before the eyes of a hundred covetous passengers, there's no state-registered watchman standing around to prevent a possible crime. Simple social control replaces repression. Mutual interest sets a dynamic in motion which requires no formalized rules. The violent are kept within bounds, the miserly are laughed at, the fearful reassured, the showoffs are mocked. In a small group of children and parents word will soon get around if a teacher is too lazy, incapable or terroristic to be put up with. Such a teacher will soon lose her customers.

I know, of course, that in our community it is considered naive to make suggestions. The idea that anything could be different from the way it is is held to be folly by those who have any say, with the result that folly can rule unchallenged. But since I have nevertheless decided to be reasonable, at least within the bounds of and for the purposes of this plea, I must deal with every conceivable serious objection, even if no one raises it. But who's going to pay for it all? That might be the question asked by someone who is taking me seriously, an imaginary person therefore. Have you thought about the cost?

Yes, I have thought about the cost. Those who should know state that around 60 per cent of public spending on the education system goes on 'personnel costs'. The remaining 40 per cent goes almost entirely on the construction and maintenance of school buildings. This huge sum can, with a few minor exceptions, be saved. On top of that there are also the subsidies for the super-fluous transport of ten million schoolchildren and the expense of a bureaucracy which serves no discernible need.

As has been said already, the existing buildings are only of limited use for human needs. The best of the older schools could perhaps be used as old people's homes or for the homeless; the overwhelming majority will, however, have to be blown up. After all, valuable plots of land in central residential areas will be freed, and low-rent subsidized housing could be built on them, if architects equal to the task could be found. A few schools could be left standing, one for each rural and urban district. From time to time, let's say once a month, pupils and teachers could meet there, to exchange experiences and make comparisons. Doubters and renegades could change groups: the event would be half party, half market. And if our truly caring state wants to have exams at all costs, then in God's name it can have them, at least for a certain transitional period. They could likewise take place within those bleak walls from which they emerged.

Forty per cent of sixty billion marks is a tidy sum of money. With it there would be no problem hiring as many teachers as are necessary for daily home visits. Our tireless educational statisticians have discovered that we must expect more than a hundred thousand teachers to be unemployed in the next few years. Apart from that, I'd like to make the point that no one, not even the most diligent educational planners, knows how many people in this country are capable of teaching other people something. State examinations are obviously no measure of that. Certain human qualities and skills play a much more important role in the 'qualification' for a teaching post than all the high-flown nonsense that so-called educational theory has to offer. A certain deprofessionalization of the teaching profession is most fervently to be desired. It is also hard to see why every future home tutor should become a civil servant for life. A 'life sentence' shouldn't be expected of every person, and not everyone will be anxious for it anyway. It would be better to look round for bare-foot and part-time teachers who, with or without a certificate, want to take on such a job. A few months will show whether they're any good, and after a couple of years it will be possible to decide whether they're worth a pension.

All right. That may all be possible with the primary schools. But how do you intend dealing with the rest, with grammar and secondary schools, or even with the colleges and universities? Do you want to blow them up, too? How do you imagine that would work? Does Helga Schneidewind's kitchen and living-room have to serve as electrical workshop, university library and physics laboratory as well?

Dear serious, therefore nonexistent listener, I reply, I didn't suggest that at all! I'm not proposing some overall educational plan to replace some other overall educational plan. So let's leave the school at home! With a project like mine (or since there are already two of us, perhaps I can say like ours), with such a project one should start small. Let's say: in a couple of villages in Eschwege rural district, near the inner German border, and somewhere in a middling-sized town in the Ruhr, with two sets of a hundred children in groups of five, who are no longer deported to school day after day. That would require forty teachers, or shall we say fifty, in case one or two fall ill or would prefer to return to the old grind. After all, we can let the dynamite for the school buildings wait, until we see how our travelling circus gets on. If things go well, then we continue on a larger scale; if it goes badly, then we'll consider where the mistakes lie.

With the parents, for example. Every teacher and every child knows that there are vain, quarrelsome and ambitious parents. Usually they only have one aim on their minds, 'success at school', which they frequently frustrate because of their own neurotic nagging. They would probably be very suspicious of teaching without terror. But as soon as it becomes clear that their children are learning at breathtaking speed and without special effort (and that is indeed what I foresee happening), their resistance will quickly falter. Perhaps it will even turn into exaggerated enthusiasm; then it will have to be carefully and firmly explained to them that their children are not the only geniuses in the world, but that we are all fantastically talented.

Other parents still dream of education in terms of status. They're the worst. Because they would prefer to lock their children up in a social ghetto as soon as possible, so that they might enjoy what such people like to call 'the right atmosphere'. Their dream would be a home tutor under whose instruction all the six-year-old dentists' children are kept to themselves, so that on no account do they learn anything about reality. It's difficult to imagine a worse fate.

Now so far no one has devised an educational plan capable of overturning class society. So a straightforward answer to the problem can't be given. We shall have to rely on the astuteness, the curiosity and the stubbornness of the children themselves, who as a rule have little desire to keep the career dreams of their parents in mind when they've only just reached the sandbox – and on the ability of the home tutor to convince even the very last dentist, with a mixture of patience, intelligence and gentle pressure, that a homogeneous milieu produces social idiots.

But when the children get bigger, when they know more and want to know even more, then we shall have to look around for specialists, for home tutors who no longer work continuously with the same group, day after day, but who take it in turns, sometimes with one group, sometimes with another, who put in a science day, analyse a business, or who can teach their own subject in English, even if it happens to be meteorology. And so on. Remember that the home tutor is always more mobile and flexible than the schoolteacher, that he's not dealing with a large class but with a small group; that the pupils, too, can move around easily and seek out with a minimum of expense and organization every place they need to visit, whether it's the physics lab, the university library or the electrical workshop.

And where will it all end? That, I'm afraid will only emerge in the course of time. And the university? Oh, the university – that would really be no loss at all. If you've stepped inside one of these concrete sheds in the last few years, then you'll have to admit that no one can stand it there any more. The professors would rather sit at home, too. They usually have very pleasant homes in attractive locations, old flats or villas, large enough for a small seminar with four or six participants.

It seems to me that you're aiming to privatize education completely.

If you want to put it like that ... I would prefer to call what I'm proposing socialization. Only I'm afraid that all these words no longer convey very much.

And what would you hope for, if a whole country decided to put your absurd plan into action?

Well, with Milly Guggemoos I'm not quite sure. Joseph would join in immediately, Edith too. I could only foresee difficulties with Rümmelein. Dog-biscuit on the other hand would be fired with enthusiasm. Head of Department Vogel would take early retirement, Bernd Bonitz would soon get used to it, Miss Wildgruber could drop her pills down the lavatory, and I can literally hear Fritzi Bauriedl exclaiming jealously: 'I could go green with envy when I think that there was nothing like that in my day.' And, yes, I would once again be in complete agreement with Fritzi Bauriedl.

*(1982)*

# 8

# Poor Little Rich Germany!

# Preliminary Sketches for a

# Study of Manners

One Sunday afternoon in July 1948 Dr. B.,* the sixty-two-year-old specialist in skin and venereal diseases, stood at his window and looked out into the back court with a sense of depression. 'My wife had gone to another part of the city to take her elderly and completely impoverished parents some bread from us ... At lunchtime we had eaten the remainder of the beans with bread – coffee and tea was used up long ago and no more to be bought ... The evenings are dark early; next winter will surely come, and of course no prospect of any wood or coal ... I was *down* like never before, truly at the end.

'Then someone rang, no knocked, at the bell-less, current-less hall door and there stood the postman and brought me your packet of coffee ... A true miracle. A fairy-tale, as I said. Precious coffee – right away, the kettle of water on the gas, although there's prison now for that too, if you use more than the ration, and brewed myself a cup of tinto, espresso, mocha! I revived, fetched a Wallace from the lending library and survived the Sunday.'

Thirty-five years later, almost to the day, in a spacious old flat in Schöneberg,† I listen to a Berlin friend's declaration of love for

---

*The poet Gottfried Benn. [Tr.]
†A district of Berlin. [Tr.]

the old capital. She sits beside a beautiful old rustic wardrobe, wearing her torn leather jerkin, beneath original graphics, and extols the grey façades, the crumbling plaster, the run-down shops in the neighbourhood, the nearby station of the elevated railway which reminds her of the stage set in a production by Klaus Michael Gruber. She finds the city's stagnation reassuring. She sees its ghetto-like characteristics as omens of a more equable, calmer future; even the smell of sulphur and brown coal that wafts over from the east seems to make her feel at home. But Hamburg or Munich! She couldn't bear those spick-and-span façades, those hideous pedestrian precincts with their glittering boutiques for a week. Everything's at once *nouveau riche* and shabby, complacent and tasteless; in a word: West German. In her mouth this expression almost takes on a touch of obscenity. In the everyday language of West Berliners it doesn't stand for anything good. It signifies a soulless Disneyland in which affluence rages.

My friend's tirade sounds familiar. Although I know she takes every opportunity for a trip to Sardinia or Crete; that she wouldn't dream of exchanging the little Alfa Romeo for her beloved elevated railway; and that the cake she offers me has reached the upper floor of KaDeWe,* which she scours with the greed of an addict, by air from Paris – I listen to her politely, laconically finish my coffee and abandon her to her belief in the moral superiority of Schöneberg and environs.

The stories from the time after the Second World War long ago took on the sepia of nostalgia. For someone who's twenty, they sound as legendary and fantastic as tales from the Thirty Years' War. The reproachful voice which grandfathers adopt doesn't exactly contribute to their credibility. ('What we had to go through! You've no idea, how easy you've got it.')

In the autumn of 1949 I travelled abroad for the first time in my life. I've never been able to forget Göteborg's market hall, a nineteenth-century iron construction. Brightly lit stalls with fruit,

---

*A Berlin department store with a spectacular food hall. [Tr.]

different cheeses, groceries, fish, poultry, confectionery from every possible country, and the people bought these 'peace-time goods' as calmly as sleepwalkers, bored, as if it was all just a matter of course. I rubbed my eyes; I didn't want to leave; after a quarter of an hour I felt sick.

I was relieved when I met a Swedish student who had no money, just like me; but it soon turned out that our ideas of poverty had nothing in common. She lived in two large rooms in a handsome late-nineteenth-century brick building. Lift, telephone, her own bath; not a stain, crack or gap to be seen; I had the impression that everything was made of brass, as if it was still 1935, or 1925, or 1915. Even those who, like the little student teacher, didn't have a bank account, had to accept the general level of comfort and pay for it. That was the standard. There were no Nissen huts here. I dimly remember the secret resentment with which I listened to her explanations. 'At home,' I said, 'you don't need to have any visiting cards printed, and it doesn't matter if you're wearing a patched jacket.'

Then there began the famous dispute about the refrigerator. At the beginning of the fifties, the Western occupation zones were full of aggrieved cultural critics. 'Before the currency reform', their works had found great resonance. 'What is a human being? – 'Can a nation be guilty?' – 'Where is the Occident going?' The booklets which bore such titles were torn out of the booksellers' hands, just like the diligent works of the nature poets. Now that the mark was worth something again, these thoughts met with massive indifference. The paying public had got something quite different into its head: the white consumer durable which overnight had become the embodiment of affluence. Just as suddenly, the meaning of the word *satt* [full up, satisfied] changed. Until the autumn of 1948 it had expressed the modest obvious longing not to be hungry. But now it was suddenly uttered with a carping, schoolmasterly intonation; its long and monotonous career as a term of abuse had begun. The never-ending lamentation about the West Germans' vulgar materialism, about the gluttony orgies of the economic miracle, about

the deeply reprehensible attitudes of a wicked and greedy population far removed from concerns of the spirit has faithfully
accompanied us through more than three decades.

The refrigerator became the emblem of this lower attitude
towards life immediately after the currency reform. Even then I
didn't quite understand what was supposed to be so offensive
about this innocent piece of furniture. If one looks at them today
in faded Neckermann mail-order catalogues the tiny tin boxes
that had to bear the whole burden of the gluttony wave look
rather modest. But only the younger generations, who didn't
have a clue anyway, can be surprised that they were a sensational
achievement for the Germans.

Anyone who wants to look at German documentary film of
the twenties, thirties and forties has to be prepared for street
battles and torchlight processions, parades and flag ceremonies.
Yet whenever the camera lingers for a moment on the figures in
the background, shows everyday life, catches family parties,
Sunday outings, factories, allotments, then the narrow, crowded,
shabby conditions in which the Germans lived come to light:
frayed cuffs, wretched homes, hungry faces. Misery did not stop
at the sharp, snobbishly drawn class lines; the poor people's
smell of margarine, barley malt coffee and moth balls had established itself deep within the 'middle class' of civil servants, shop-
keepers, artisans and white-collar workers. This nation certainly
possessed highly advanced industries, but had to count every
penny three times. Without the promise that it would abolish
this want, even if only by pillage and invasion, Fascism would
never have won. What it left behind, apart from forty million
dead, was a totally impoverished country.

It hardly seems to require an explanation that after 1945 the
Germans applied all their energies to escaping their material
miseries, the old traditional one just as much as the new one they
had brought upon themselves. On the contrary, what is remarkable is that they have never been able to get over the success of
this project. Affluence seems to weigh on the souls of the Federal
Republic's citizens like a mute reproach. At least that must be
the conclusion of anyone who relies on published opinion. How

far that is to be trusted is another question. I fear that those who keep dinning the critique of affluence in people's ears themselves share in this affluence.

The best and most elementary reason for this German ambivalence was a bad conscience. Such an impulse never had greater justification than in the years after the defeat. It was indeed difficult to grasp that after their Fascist crimes, after a devastating war which was their own doing, the Germans, at least in the West, were to be rich for the first time in their history, as a reward, so to speak. It amounted to a moral scandal which any halfway sensitive nature could not so easily cope with.

Anyone who appeals to the guilt feelings of others must inevitably expect questions to be asked of his own. The conservative cultural criticism of the fifties, however, had conspicuously little interest in inquiring into its own historical conscience. It preferred to enter the debate on poverty and wealth with its two favourite fears, namely (a) the loss of values and (b) the onslaught of mass man.

In solemn tones these gentlemen drew to our attention that the German dazzled by the prospect of an all too comfortable life was in danger of forfeiting a feeling for the higher things and the capacity for abstinence. What was to become of his traditional virtues: a sense of duty and thriftiness, love of fatherland and discipline, loyalty and a spirit of sacrifice? Did the new wealth, embodied by the refrigerator, not threaten to extinguish that 'still inner glory' of which the poet speaks? An anxious shaking of heads was unavoidable in the face of such risks.

As far as mass man was concerned, he, as was his nature, ensured further indignation. Wealth in itself was not objectionable, as long as it remained where it belonged, that is, in cultivated, responsible hands. Now, however, a completely unrestrained, pleasure-seeking populace was setting out *en masse* for the Baltic coast or Majorca. One was no longer safe from hoi polloi anywhere. The so-called selfish society was putting forth its first blooms: cleaning women were greedy for radios with magic eyes and golden moulding, dustmen first bought themselves Goggomobiles, then Volkswagens. What leered out from the advertisements at the professors and leader-writers of those distant days was, it is true, only a spectre; but even the spectre of equality was enough to strike fear into them. Unlike the more intelligent fractions of their class, the cultural critics just didn't have the faintest idea of the charms of a prolonged consumer boom; they simply couldn't grasp that increasing private consumption had become the most important driving force of German capitalism.

This was exactly what the ideologists of the New Left had understood very well when in the mid-sixties they tore the torch of the critique of affluence out of the hands of the sour old gentlemen in order to bear it to new shores. For them, the diabolical aspect of our brand new wealth was that it drove the condition of exploitation and alienation in which we languished to an extreme without us even knowing what was happening to us. In vain did competent authorities try to explain to us the difference between true and false needs. The working class in particular, no sooner had the refrigerator been installed, energetically demanded the deep freeze, the washing machine and the Beetle; and an end to this robust appetite for newer and newer toys was not in sight. How the New Left understood so well that these needs were, without exception, false, is unknown. Did they perhaps owe this knowledge to the enlightened but strict teachers' and ministers' families in which so many of them had grown up? The origin of their judgements was obscure, but they were uncompromisingly expressed. The full shop windows, the bargain special offers, the cheap holidays: it was all not simply lies and fraud, it was pure terror. It was consistent then, that a department store had to serve as the first beacon of the 'armed struggle' in Germany.* The 'masses' were confused. They just could not get it into their heads that the political vanguard wanted to spare them the fatal

---

*The first act of what was to become in RAF (Red Army Faction) was the attempted arson of a Frankfurt store. [Tr.]

blancmange mix, the idiotic five-gear racing bike, the perfidious electric blanket and the repulsive twenty-seven-piece coffee set. But this lack of insight was easily explained. The people were simply dulled by years of manipulation, and by this time it had become difficult, not to say impossible, to distinguish the glorious working class from a crowd of incorrigible consumer idiots.

Like the cultural conservatives before them, the critics of affluence from the extra-parliamentary opposition also suffered from a problem which is perhaps related to the shape of the human body: they found it difficult to see as far as the end of their nose. It's true that the New Left liked to talk about refusal, but they spent whole nights in the repertory cinemas. The spaghetti western was their staple diet, the television stayed on until the end of transmission in the communes, and it was not only for reasons of mimicry that the armed fighters at times displayed a conspicuous taste for fast cars, fast clothes and fast money.

The justifications changed, the anger against wealth remained. Yet another ten years passed – by this time no one was satisfied with refrigerators any more, by now it was flights to Bangkok and Mombasa, surf-boards and house-buying – and for the first time an argument against the German religion of accumulation appeared that held water: the commandment of ecological reason. Now that growth rates were sinking and energy costs were climbing up and up, the old sense of unease could suddenly rely on new, solid facts. The alternative protest culture even went so far as to pick up the broom of criticism and sweep in front of its own door. Established lawyers who decorated their VW Golfs with the assertion that they were energy savers were sighted. More radical spirits went one step further: they devised ways of living in which an uncomfortable future was tested even before it had begun. Since that time there are Germans, even if not very many, who have opted for a life in sackcloth and ashes. They live in stables, speak the dialect of prison and camp inmates, go around in rags and sleep on old mattresses.

Yet something ambiguous clings to the figure of the drop-out. His poverty is staged. For this reason alone his choice cannot be generalized. Those who have no choice, for example the almost two and a half million recipients of social security in the Federal Republic, will probably have the least inclination to follow his example. Presumably most of them would prefer to get on the bus today rather than tomorrow, if they could afford the ticket.

The only people who are always right when they castigate wealth are the poor. Their criticism is unambiguous, and it can only be contradicted by practice. However, it aims to abolish poverty, not wealth. Whether by collective or individual effort, millions of Germans have attained this goal in the last thirty-five years. As far as I know, no one has yet attempted to write a social history of the Federal Republic which described soberly and in detail this stubborn, fantastic, utterly fragmented class struggle.

'The bourgeoisie,' says *The Communist Manifesto*, 'has left remaining no other nexus between man and man than naked self-interest, than "callous cash payment".' But what is set down there as accomplished fact was from the beginning an unrealizable dream and nightmare, a project condemned to failure. In reality capitalism can only exist on condition that it forgoes enforcing its principle. A world which reduces all human relations to 'callous cash payment' has, of course, never existed, for the simple reason that the most important services of all are largely offered free of charge (even if by no means out of pure charity). Pregnancy, bringing up children and housework are all beyond price. Other forms of exchange, like mutual aid, hospitality, giving presents and inheritance are much older than capitalism. Every modern economic system would collapse overnight if it only permitted transactions which depended on the calculation of profit.

Unpaid services have always been the stepchild of economics. They don't appear in any calculation of gross national product, in any growth or incomes statistics. Recent American research has shown that the 'turnover' of this unknown sector can easily match that of the official economy. And the non-monetary transfers are by no means withering away with increasing modernization. The opposite is the case. In societies which have passed the stage of primitive accumulation, their volume is growing more rapidly than wealth as a whole.

What is social wealth anyway? Big question. In terms of theory the concept is fairly unclear; in practice it's indispensable if one wants to describe the economic condition of the Federal Republic. For the prosperity of this country can no longer be understood as the private property of a constantly shrinking class of capitalists. It certainly remains true that ever fewer people dispose of an ever larger share of productive assets; an end to this process of concentration is not in sight. But while the rich are getting richer, the reverse is not true. The great polarization, which Marxist theory has prophesied for over a hundred years has not taken place. The petty bourgeoisie doesn't have the least intention of allowing itself to be proletarianized. On the contrary, its hegemony determines West German society, in its obsessions as much as its ephemeral fashions. The *middle class* would also like to see social wealth shaped and distributed in its own image: neatly, cleanly and according to strict rules. But that requires non-monetary transfer services to be taken over by the state to a large extent. The per capita tax load rises, of course, and an enormous distributive bureaucracy comes into being to administer this wealth. The traditional political advocate of such redistributive processes is Social Democracy; yet today only very hard-nosed conservative circles dream of reversing this process. There will be no reprivatization of social wealth, even after a change of government. State control of prosperity is irreversible by parliamentary means.

This is evident above all in this country's extravagantly developed infrastructure, from the motorway to the public swimming pool, from the comprehensive school to the local passenger transport network. But these tangible signs of collective wealth provide only a feeble idea of the total quantity of transfer payments, grants, subsidies, fringe benefits, which the state, like some thousand-armed Buddha, gives and takes. Every such measure comes to be taken for granted from the moment it is introduced. A few arbitrarily chosen examples: every school pupil today has available a computer capacity which the CIA couldn't even dream of thirty years ago. Spa cures are available to everyone.. Every theatre seat is subsidized to the tune of eighty marks. And so on. This state of affairs annoys some people. Others don't even notice that they're privileged simply by living in this country.

One curious consequence of this floating wealth is that the fetish value of commodities is decreasing. This is clear from the example of the telephone. Its social prestige is greatest when only a very exclusive circle have it; its use value, on the other hand, increases with the number of subscribers. Only when everyone can call everyone else has the network achieved its greatest utility – a situation the Federal Republic comes closer to every year. But as the level of saturation increases so the irrational marginal utility tends to decline. Ostentatious consumption is no longer regarded with envy and admiration but with a shrug of the shoulders.

It's a pity that the Germans don't have a Balzac or even a Zola to record and pass on their morals and customs. The luxuriant varieties of adaptation and compromise which Social Democratic wealth produces outside the arena of ritual distributive struggles, the curious blooms which thrust up in the hothouse of the Federal Republic could supply material for every kind of comedy. A few of these phenomena will have to serve, however inadequately, as examples.

1. *Finding a niche.* Werner F., a qualified librarian, an otherwise inconspicuous man, has a single all-consuming passion; he loves the cinema. However, he doesn't think much of what television and the film theatres have to offer. True cinema, he believes, has been dead since 1930: the sound film destroyed it. Werner F. has seen most silent films of which a copy still exists. He has compiled a complete catalogue of every film shown publicly in Germany before 1930. His archive does not only include production credits and posters. He has also tracked down all the film criticism from the beginning and documented it bibliographically. One might have thought that such extensive

research would only be possible at an institute of higher education. However, F. has never had an academic appointment – presumably his attitude to cinema was not orthodox enough for such a career. Instead he earns his living as a librarian with the army. I could even name his posting and department; only I don't see why I should put the audit court on his back. Because, with the tacit consent of his superiors, F. has all the technical resources of a well-equipped army at his disposal for these exotic researches: fax machines, microfiches, data banks, photographic laboratories, computers, copiers. In short, he has found a sociological niche and in his own modest way turned swords to ploughshares.

Not all niche-dwellers display such impressive productivity. Many content themselves with driving through Africa in an old VW bus for a couple of months, or they play the fiddle in the country, or they re-train, or go back to university. What distinguishes all niche-dwellers is a certain careless virtuosity, a limitless contempt for every official career and a complete absence of guilt. They make their way through the jungle of the institutions with marvellous agility, they settle in the shelter provided by guidelines and feed on grants and subsidies.

Such a way of life often arouses the resentment of older people. Nothing but work-shy, good-for-nothing parasites, one hears it said, who want to have an easy life at other people's expense. The example of Werner F., who even spends his Sundays bent over old catalogues, shows this isn't necessarily true. Besides, it's well known that work has become a scarce resource. For that reason alone the Federal Republic has no other choice but to feed hundreds of thousands, if not millions of niche-dwellers. The good nature with which that happens stands in strange contrast to the usual lament about the soulless indifference which it supposedly exhibits. All the same, it's less a spontaneous impulse of the heart than a systematic necessity, and that's why I hardly believe that the gentlemen with the social lawnmower will succeed in 'cutting down abuses' and 'cutting back undergrowth.'

2. *The smart guys.* During the founding years of the Bonn republic, tax was a subject which only interested the top 50,000. Today, on the other hand, anyone who has a regular income at all, including the slater and the Turkish immigrant labourer, is confronted by a mass of fiscal regulations before which he would have to capitulate were there not a tax consultant and an income tax association on every street corner. Everyone knows: the system is not only opaque, it is unjust, inconsistent, abstruse. Anyone who doesn't know his way around it gets robbed. The consequence is that the country has become populated by millions of dodgers and fiddlers. 'Deductible allowances' have become a national mania. Whole branches of business, like gastronomy and house-building owe their existence to them. Even if the leading achievements of the big companies are unrivalled and unattainable in this area (one could call a man like Flick the von Karajan of fiddling), there can be no doubt that everyman emulates them as best he can. Every taxi receipt counts, every 'asset-creating expenditure', all the 'luncheon expenses' [*Mehrverpflegungsaufwand*], every 'tax deduction for professionals', and every 'exceptional depreciation of lower-value movable items of equipment subject to wear and tear', even if it's only a matter of a guitar or a scooter.

The tax payers' tropical fictions in turn provide a living for a thousand-headed army of editors and reviewers who, as consultants, refine the text, and as tax inspectors try to distinguish between fantastic invention and documentary social reportage. The coloured questionnaires of the tax department have become the Federal Republic's most popular literary genre.

3. *Occult money.* Our Charlie is one of those people who can claim, with a completely guileless expression, that they don't understand why there's so much fuss about money. 'I don't need anything,' he says, and that's the simple truth. First, he only wanted to stay one, maybe two nights, but then ... the back room in the communal flat was empty anyway, since Katja moved out, and at least our Charlie looks after the cat. Things only get difficult if he drives down to Tuscany for a few weeks

again to look after the farmhouse of an acquaintance of an acquaintance. He only wants to do the owner, a director of advertising films, a favour; otherwise, if the house were unlived in, he would have to worry about his antique toy railway. We don't know who actually gave Charlie the battered Opel in which he drives down. Recently he turned up with a huge refrigerator when ours was broken; he got it for nothing, in return for taking it away, from four flights up; it just shows you that when something has to be done, Charlie can pitch in too. His therapy is paid for by his uncle in Belgium, import–export trade; at the Frankfurt Fair Charlie told him about his problems with work and his depressions. He takes his shirts – Charlie puts on fresh clothes every day – to Katja, who has a washing machine; and if he really needs some money, then he just has to see Siegfried Ochs, who's stuck with his M.A. thesis. After all, one day Siegfried Ochs is going to take over his father's brewery; he's happy to hand over a couple of 100-mark notes if Charlie writes him a clever introduction and a lengthy bibliography. No need to worry! Our Charlie who, like a hundred thousand others, needs nothing, never has any money unless it's occult money, will get by.

And yet even our friend Charlie can't cope without his therapy which has been dragging on for an astonishingly long time now. We're worried about him. Sometimes he wonders what the point of everything is, and if we can't give him an answer, then he curses the Federal Republic all evening. If we didn't like our Charlie so much, we know all the things we'd like to throw at him.

The hatred of affluence, we would say in a cutting voice, is one of the lies by which the West German intelligentsia lives; it's a moral alibi. It finds it difficult to live down the fact that compared to its English, French, Italian neighbours, it has a pretty easy life. But a bad conscience isn't very fruitful, at best it produces stratagems to relieve or displace the burden, and at worst self-deception and hypocrisy. Apart from that, in Germany such spasms are as foreign to those who wield political and economic power as they are to those who have to live on a weekly wage. One knows just as well as the other that money alone doesn't make people unhappy.

After thirty years it would perhaps not be a bad idea to analyse social wealth and its consequences soberly and without the usual subterfuges. But anyone who wants to understand it, shouldn't wait too long. Because it really looks as if its days are numbered. No one who has ever opened an atlas or a Bible can be surprised at that. The preacher in Ecclesiastes knew long ago that wealth is always the exception and never the rule: an extremely improbable, exceedingly unstable state, an historical extravagance only those who believe in miracles can expect to be permanent. To others, the transience of our morals may suffice as a comfort. Personally, I don't believe it's more dangerous to have a full stomach than to be hungry. Let's not exaggerate! Our wealth, this tenacious mayfly, won't last so very much longer! If things are still going relatively well for us then we should be able to bear that fate with a little detachment, with a touch of irony.

*(1982)*

# 9

## On the Irresistibility of the

## Petty Bourgeoisie:

## A Sociological Caprice

The fact that you are reading this is in itself proof that you're one of them. Sorry, dear reader, for addressing you so directly. (And perhaps 'proof' is too strong a word.) I concede that in what follows I intend to state more than I can prove – e.g., that there is such a thing as the petty bourgeoisie – and without batting an eyelid. After all, *petty bourgeoisie* is a term like any other, though it may sound a little archaic (like *dear reader*), and it's not my fault that it is usually pronounced in an irritated tone – in fact, almost spat out. This was always so, ever since about 1830, when Ludwig Börne, himself petty bourgeois, introduced it into the political vocabulary of Germans.

Unscrupulously – i.e., without having pored over the tens of thousands of pages on the concept of class in M., E., and X. – I furthermore assert that the class dealt with here can be defined only *ex negativo*, namely as that class which is neither . . . nor . . .

Not out of curiosity, but only in the hope of making myself understood, I take the liberty of asking a few questions.

Do you, or could you, live on the returns from capital that you have invested in the means of production?

No?

Exactly as I suspected.

Does this mean that you live exclusively by selling your work by the hour to a capitalist?

Yes? Are you sure?

So you have no scholarships? No interest? Fees? Subsidies?

Charge account? Profit margins and equities? Royalties? Rents? Bonuses? Commissions?

No accumulated educational capital? No allowance from home? No guaranteed employment? No real estate? No means of production of your own; not even a personal reference library? In short, no income derived from surplus value created by others?

Once again, I beg your pardon for asking these pedantic, impertinent questions.

Possibly it is not the thing itself that bothers you so much as the term. It sounds so pitiful: *petty bourgeoisie*. Truly, you would not be the only one embarrassed. That is why those whom I mean by this term (of whom I count myself a part) have invented a swarm of other names for it. Please look through the list and simply check off the ones you like:

1. Middle class (old, new, upper, lower, middle, 'cultured').
2. White collar (middle, upper, etc.).
3. Civil servants, other 'employees', bureaucracy.
4. Managers, 'specialists', technocrats, technical intelligentsia.
5. The 'self-employed', 'free' professions.
6. 'Graduates', the intelligentsia ('freelance', scientific, etc.).

So you see, no one is trying to step on your toes. You are merely invited, if at all possible, to feel that it applies to you and are asked to permit me, for simplicity's sake, to use the first person plural. Thank you.

So we belong to a class that neither controls nor owns what matters, the famous means of production, and that does not produce what also matters, the famous surplus value (or perhaps produces it only indirectly and incidentally – a point often heatedly debated in seminars, but by far not as sore a point as this might lead us to believe). This is precisely what is so imprecise. The petty bourgeoisie is not one of the main parties in the (famous) main contradiction; it is neither the ruling class nor the exploited one, but the in-between class, left over, the fluctuating remnant.

A remnant embarrassing to bear, especially for those who love nice, neat, simple worldviews. For the fluctuating class is always the disturbing one. Its existence always injects confusion into theory and practice. In the last hundred years, therefore, there has been no lack of attempts to eliminate the petty bourgeoisie – in order to remove this scandal from the face of the earth (and for a whole gamut of other reasons which we will perhaps deal with later). To a certain extent, it was said, this task could be left to the (iron) laws of history. All by itself it was (and here and there still is) said, a part of this class – the smaller part – will join the side of the goats, will rise to the ranks of capitalism, and consequently will perish with it, for it is doomed; the other part, of course the far greater one, will rejoin the sheep and there reap the fruits of socialism: for these just men would, because of the (famous) laws governing the movement of capital, become proletarianized, though not always voluntarily. Then the minuscule little remnant of the unjust would have to be induced to disappear. Our fore-fathers, if they belonged to the class we are denouncing, heard the message and ardently believed the prophecy with fear and trembling.

It did not come true. Whatever may have become of the petty bourgeoisie, its apocalypse has not arrived. Neither the progressive concentration of capital nor worldwide inflation, neither scientific and technical progress nor wars and crises have finished it off. Not even the introduction of a sort of socialism has succeeded in eliminating the fluctuating class in the Soviet Union, in Eastern Europe and in Third World countries. On the contrary, it has produced a new type of petty bourgeois, the petty bourgeois of the victorious revolution, its bosses, cadres, function-aries; strange mutants, weird specimens of a 'new class' that looks very much like the old one.

But even in capitalist societies, the good old, the bad old petty bourgeois has not remained unchanged. The Biedermeier figures of the little craftsman, the shop owner, the pedant and the dignitaries no longer play the main role as they once did (though a look at German parliaments shows that this type has not died out completely). The 'middle class' has, however, apparently

made up for its losses quite easily. Indeed, as tough and as unob-
trusive as grass, it has even expanded quantitatively. With every
structural change in society it apparently sent forth new runners.
In the scientific transformation of production, the growth of
tertiary and quaternary sectors of the economy, the tremendous
enlargement of private and public administrations, the expansion of the consciousness industry, of educational and medical
institutions – the petty bourgeoisie was always there. After every
political revolution it has immediately installed itself in the newly
created state and party organizations, and not only defended its
social 'inventory' but even expanded it.

At present, there seems to be no theory to explain the power to
survive, the influence and the historical success of this class. An
explanation is still needed even for the fact that the petty bourgeoisie has been crudely and stubbornly underestimated for at
least 150 years. No one has contributed more to this low opinion
than the petty bourgeoisie itself. This is certainly connected with
its peculiar class consciousness. It was broken in spirit from the
first, and today can only be described as a sheer vacuum. For just
as the class can be defined only in negative terms so its understanding of itself is also negative. The petty bourgeois wants to be
anything but petty bourgeois. He tries to gain his identity not by
allegiance to his class, but by separating himself off from it and
denying it. But what links him with his own kind is just what he
contests: the petty bourgeois is always someone else. This
strange self-hatred acts as a cloak of invisibility. With its help the
class as a whole has made itself almost invisible. Solidarity and
collective action are out of the question for it; it will never attain
the self-consciousness of a distinct class. The mechanism of
repression leads subjectively to its not being taken seriously as a
social entity, and objectively it prevents the formation of clearly
defined, comprehensive political class organizations. The social
image of the petty bourgeoisie is inclined to mimicry; the more
this class grows, the less recognizable it becomes.

Such a divided and fragmented class has probably never
existed before. The extreme objective and subjective fragment-

ation of the petty bourgeoisie is not puzzling. It follows logically from its economic situation and its history. Its relationship to the means of production has always been derivative and indirect. This leads, on the one hand, to an inability to seize political power. This class cannot and does not become the ruling class, and even this impotence is strangely internalized. The petty bourgeois both rejects power and adores it, which means that he delegates it and accepts it only as it is delegated to him to administer, justify and doubt. But the smaller the actual dominant class becomes, the more it needs the petty bourgeoisie to transmit and impose its rule on the general public. Otherwise the working class would long ago have ceased to remain disarmed and held in check. So even the political influence of the petty bourgeoisie must be defined in negative terms as a sort of inarticulated power of veto. This explains petty bourgeois interest in the formal aspect of politics, in procedures, regulations, legalistic rules and forms of communication.

But this inability to unify and organize has another side. The class's many-sidedness, its infinitesimally graduated articulation by status, professional group and ownership is also the basis of its tenacity, dynamism and aggressiveness. It is an advantage in social evolution, a factor of self-preservation. In biological systems there is a general rule that a species is all the harder to eradicate the greater its variability, its genetic pool. An analogous rule of thumb applies to society. A social monolith finds it harder to survive changes of historical conditions than a complex articulated assemblage. Adaptability, ideologically depreciated and denounced by the petty bourgeois as characterless opportunism, certainly increases a class's chances for survival. And no one has this to a higher degree than the petty bourgeois. No social niche is so small, so remote, so exposed that he would not try to occupy it. Never to take a final stand, and to seize every possibility: those are the only lessons that the class has learned from its variegated history.

Long ago it abandoned its former social character, the leisurely, sheltered comfort and smugness of its first great period. How deep this predilection for self-satisfied conservatism really went is, incidentally, still open to question: even the old petty bourgeoisie of the nineteenth century was nervous, irritable, easily incensed and outraged, with a sporadic inclination to radicalism, sudden excitement, critical out of *ressentiment* and courageous out of fear. It was men of the petty bourgeoisie who developed the stereotype of the smug Philistine; and the *Bohème*, whose speciality was to alarm other petty bourgeois, was also recruited mainly from the petty bourgeoisie.

Today the class is swarming with men of progress, and no one is more avid than they to adopt the latest trend. It is always up to date. No one can more quickly change ideologies, clothing, forms of communication and habits than the petty bourgeois. He is a new Proteus, capable of learning to the point of losing all identity. Always fleeing from the archaic, he is always chasing himself.

Political defeats can shake the working class in its class consciousness; but it can never be robbed of the calm conviction of the necessity of its existence. Even the capitalists consider themselves indispensable. The petty bourgeoisie, on the other hand, has to incessantly struggle with the feeling of being superfluous. Cynicism is a privilege of the ruling class. But the supplanting class tries to justify itself; it is permanently in quest of meaning. It is just as resourceful as it is unscrupulous, yet always in need of morality. In rationalization and doubt its mastery is unequalled. But its self-criticism and self-denial are of limited scope. A class cannot abolish itself. Thus doubt and ruin serve the petty bourgeoisie ultimately as an incentive and pleasure. To make it feel insecure is child's play. To wean it of itself is absolutely impossible. The petty bourgeoisie always questions itself; it is the experimental class *par excellence*. But the process of its struggle against itself serves only to preserve and expand its own sphere. There's a method to its insecurity: it is a purposeful strategy always pursuing the chimera of security.

How can the central position occupied by the petty bourgeoisie in all highly industrialized modern societies be explained? Our class has neither capital nor direct access to the means of production; it is as far removed from political and economic power as ever. Does it really not know the basis of its own strength. Or is it merely too timid to let the cat out of the bag? The answer is obvious, simple and brief: the petty bourgeoisie today has cultural hegemony in all highly industrialized societies. It has become the exemplary class, the only one that produces the forms of daily life on a mass scale and imposes them on everybody else. It brings about innovation. It determines what is considered good and worth striving for. It decides what people think. (The dominant ideas are no longer those of the ruling class but those of the petty bourgeoisie.) It invents ideologies, sciences, technologies. It dictates what morals and psychology mean. It decides what goes on in so-called private life. It is the only class that produces art and fashion, philosophy and architecture, criticism and design.

The entire area of mass consumption is decisively shaped by the ideas of the petty bourgeoisie. Brand-names and advertisements are projections of its consciousness. In consumption, all features of the social character of the petty bourgeoisie are rediscovered in generalized form: dynamics and individualization, progress as a flight forward, formalism and constant innovation, superfluity and the need for demarcation. It is enough to point out the form of the two consumer goods that are emblematic for our civilization: the television set and the private automobile. Only the petty bourgeoisie could have thought up these two remarkable objects.

Similarly impressive are his achievements in the field of immaterial production. The organizations of the superstructure on all sides are occupied by members of our class, and practically all 'schools', 'trends', and 'movements' that play a part in highly industrialized societies have been inspired, supported and implemented by the petty bourgeoisie: from tourism to do-it-yourself, from the artistic avant-garde to urban studies, from the student movement to ecology, from cybernetics to the feminist movement, from organized sports to 'sexual liberation', and so on and so forth. Every alternative impulse within our culture has been appropriated and absorbed by the petty bourgeoisie – one need only recall the example of rock music, which originally was an autonomous expression of young proletarians, just as jazz had been fifty years before. Even originally subversive ideologies such as anarchism and Marxism have today, for the most part, been requisitioned by the petty bourgeoisie.

How the 'experimental class' arrived at its cultural hegemony could be explained only after a detailed materialistic investigation. A high level of industrialization is surely a necessary, though perhaps not sufficient, condition. The model of petty bourgeois culture presupposes a certain social wealth. Only when production is highly organized can the social area of distribution, circulation and management expand so much that a broad 'middle class' results. And, vice versa, only with increasing centralization and concentration does the ruling class shrink so much that it loses its cultural hegemony.

The frenetic productivity of the petty bourgeoisie and its capacity for innovation should, however, be explained simply from the fact that it has no choice. It is 'intelligent', 'talented', 'inventive' because its survival depends on it. The power-holders do not need this: they hire others to invent, they buy intelligence and 'train' talented people. But any autonomous productivity is systematically driven out of the proletariat. 'You're not supposed to think!' bellowed F.W. Taylor, petty bourgeois and the father of efficiency expertise, at the production workers. And this is how things have stood of course not only in the West. So the fabulous talent of the petty bourgeoisie, like most of its other qualities, is explained *ex negativo*.

But what makes the hegemonic culture of the petty bourgeoisie so irresistible is quite another question. How could it become the universal model emulated by billions of people? What is distinctive about this model? By virtue of what qualities does it, both on a national and a worldwide scale, eliminate all alternative designs?

That the European proletariat is shaped by petty bourgeois culture in its life-style and aspirations is evident. But the old way of life of the capitalists has also been completely abolished: its luxury has shrunk to the format of illustrated magazines; its 'exclusive' standard is now merely that of those petty bourgeois who can afford a more expensive brand. On the other hand, it is only a matter of time before the electric toothbrush makes its triumphal entry into the slums. And even today there is no Oriental bazaar, no Malayan or Caribbean market where the advanced fossils of petty bourgeois culture have not long since overcome all resistance. The economic causes of this universal penetration are well known; the petty bourgeoisie did not create them. But the cultural dimension of this process outdoes every purely economic perspective. (Pier Paolo Pasolini has described it masterfully for Italy.)

So the question remains: what is so unique, so seductive, about the table cigarette lighter, the Pepsodent taste, concrete poetry, a hobby room, Sesame Street, the plastic lemon, opinion polls, *Emanuelle*, deodorants, sensitivity training, the Polaroid camera, veneers, parapsychology, 'Peanuts', metal-plating, sports shirts, science fiction, airplane-hijacking, the digital watch – that from Kamchatka to Tierra del Fuego no one, no nation and no class, is immune to them? Is there really no antidote to whatever our class dreams up? Will no one, not even the Congolese, be spared from wearing underpants designed by a French fashion designer? Must the Vietnamese also gulp down Valium? Is there no escape from behaviour therapy, Concorde, Masters & Johnson, suburban neighbourhoods, and curriculum research? And this furniture upholstered in air-breathing, dirt resistant, rich, leather-look vinyl, with reversible seat and back cushions of polyurethane foam, button-tufted, with cotton-padded, no-sag springs, decorative buckles and cedar-base, which rolls and turns on chrome-plated casters, this stupendously beautiful, low-priced, unit-constructed piece pursues me relentlessly and prowls after me like the hedgehog in the fairy-tale, and is always there ahead of me at the birthday party, on TV, in the two-room apartment of a Turkish worker in Berlin-Schöneberg, in *Der Spiegel*, at the dentist's office, on any adventure holiday, in the offices of the responsible party organizations, in a special sale, on the beautiful blue Danube, at the White House, and on the trash heap – will it, no matter what, always roll on irresistibly, this incarnation of all our class's beautiful dreams, until it has reached the Souks of Damascus and the Shanghai airport? Probably it got there long ago.

*(1976)*

# 10

## In Defence of Normality

Normally I would never have got mixed up in something like that ... On the other hand, I think it's quite normal for him not to put up with it for ever ... Under normal circumstances the motion would have been carried without opposition ... The situation in Nicaragua has returned to normal ... Anyone of normal intelligence would agree ... I've always told you that Gudrun's behaviour isn't quite normal.

*Normal/abnormal*: it is hardly possible to think of either of these terms without immediately being referred to the other, and then in such a manner as if the two simply excluded one another. Caught between the Freudian unconscious, Marxian economics and Nietzsche's Will to Power, normality does not have a good name in contemporary philosophy. The perverse is preferred to the holy, the abnormal to the normal, madness to banality.

Normality always seems to have its point of reference in the existing order of things; to that extent it possesses neither the charms of disobedience nor the creative virtues of innovation. But such a dichotomy makes the matter too easy; for whether one becomes an MP or a wolf man one cannot become either without transgressing a norm; even Victor d'Aveyron, the 'wild child', even Einstein, only became what they are by submitting to a particular social medium, which swallowed, tamed, drilled, educated them ...

*Enciclopedia Einaudi*, Vol. IX
(entry on *normale/anormale*), Turin 1979

Mrs Gretel S., seventy, divorced, two grown-up sons, a younger brother, by profession 'daily help', pension amounts to 384 marks a month, says: 'I could live anywhere if I had to.' Political views: 'Always the same shit.' Basically works without declaring anything; 'I can't afford taxes, I've got my children to think about' (debts, hire purchase, alimony, etc.).

Possesses an outstanding knowledge of bourgeois society, diagnoses marriage crises, stinginess, alcoholism, adultery, opportunism, property relations, etc. at a single glance. Is not at all afraid of catastrophes, but is prepared at all times for the outbreak of a war. 'Always had what I needed, even after being bombed out: butter, French cognac, bed linen, everything.'

Tends towards redistribution: if clothes hangers are needed she quietly brings clothes hangers from houses which have too many clothes hangers. Extremely tidy, regards dirt as a personal enemy, so has ideal qualifications for her profession. Ideologically unpredictable, from time to time repeats phrases from the Weimar Republic, from the Third Reich, from the post-war years, from *Bild* newspaper; yet she ruthlessly employs this material to her own ends, so that her constructions resemble a series of ad hoc shacks erected overnight with planks stolen from ruined buildings, torn down again in the morning. Overall impression: anarchic spontaneity.

Sleeps from seven in the evening until four in the morning, then listens to the radio in bed. 'If there's a war, I'll go to the Stubai Valley on foot. An old friend of mine, a hotel-owner, always has a spare bed for me. My advice is to hold on to a kilo of pepper, I can get that for you cheaply. Pepper is always the first thing that runs out, then you barter that for meat from the butcher, butter from the farmer. One kilo can get you through a whole year.'

The concept of normality is a terminological pudding, a pulplike mass which sets hard when one's not looking but remains wobbly and falls apart as soon as it is approached with a sharp instrument. Trying to define it is a hopeless task. You've made your normality, now you must live with it.

The conceptual ABC to be found in the reference books – primary and secondary socialization, repression, early childhood impressions, white pedagogy, black pedagogy, training, social mediation – has itself now become pudding-like, is itself already normality.

Little Historical Dictionary for describing the ordinary person:*

The ordinary man/woman in the street, the little man, the ordinary consumer, the man on the Clapham omnibus, the average person.

Commonplace, common, plain, ordinary-looking, narrow-minded, passive, apathetic, routine.

Conformist, Philistine, backwoodsman, suburban, without a mind of his own.

Vulgar materialism, parochial horizon, low-brow.

Mass man, consumer idiot, one of the crowd.

Inarticulate, lower instincts, conformist.

Scum of the earth, flock of sheep, dull mass.

Carried along by the crowd, vulgar, short-sighted, manipulated.·

Employees, labour force, manpower, labouring masses, workers by hand and brain.

Comrades, colleagues, brothers.

Fug, fustiness, petty bourgeoisie, silent majority.

Ordinary people, simple people, common people, rabble, mob.

---

*In English 'ordinary' tends to carry the deprecatory connotations which in German are conveyed by 'normal'. [Tr.]

Reversing these designations provides a self-portrait of the person who has invented them. Whoever defines the normal, ordinary person, whoever decides who is and who is not a normal person would be (among other things) active, sensitive, articulate, independent, complicated; would think far ahead, would let himself be guided by noble motives, would live far from the world of consumption in a sphere of leisure, of contemplation; would be touched by greatness; would not appear as one of a crowd, large or small, but always only in the singular, and only one thing could with certainty be said about him: under no circumstances would he be ordinary, common or conformist.

Self-quotation I: To a Man in the Tram Car

Why? I don't want to know about you, man
with the watery eyes, with the parting
of fat and straw, briefcase full of cheese.
No. I don't care for you. You don't smell good.
There are too many of you. On the staircase your gaze
behind the counters is everywhere in front of the cinemas,
in the mirror a greedy face smeared with soap.
And you too (not even hate) turn away
to the walnut cabinets, to Sophia Loren,
go home covered in sweat, full of aspidistras
and diapers.

> *Verteidigung der Wölfe* ('The Wolves Defended Against
> the Lambs'), Frankfurt 1957

I haven't the faintest idea who the first person to damn normality was; but I shouldn't be too surprised if it was a poet. (*Odi profanum vulgus et arceo* – after all, that's two thousand years old already.) Presumably what he wanted to let his fellow human-beings know was the following.

It doesn't even occur to me to mention myself and you and those like you in the same breath. In future please regard me as an outsider. Polite as I am, I should like to leave the question open as to whether I merely stand outside normality or whether I am far above it. In any case, I should like to ask you to take account of the fact that I am a dangerous, holy, subversive person, who is far from ready to abide by your habits, rules and agreements. You love security, I love risk; you are satisfied with *common sense*, I am concerned with a much higher meaning. And please, if that doesn't suit you, go ahead and persecute me with your vulgar vindictiveness, your secret envy, you can stone me or poison me. Please don't restrain yourselves. By treating me differently from the others, by treating me worse, in fact, you yourselves provide the proof – if any proof was still needed – that I'm not one of you, not part of the common crowd.

Thus far the speech of the hypothetical, unknown writer who invented the outsider game. As with all good inventions, word of this one spread very quickly, and it is, if I may be allowed to use the expression, quite normal that it did not long remain the sole property of this unique individual. Disciples clung to his heels, imitators, fans who one and all declined to belong to the vulgar mob and who took it as an insult if someone accused them to their face of being quite normal, ordinary people.

In time, the situation grew ever more critical. For whole schools, cliques, factions and parties formed which claimed to stand outside every kind of normality. They had to have their own bars, their own clubs, publishing houses, exhibitions, journals, museums, holiday villages, clothes shops, restaurants. Whole crowds of bohemians, *décadents* and Dadaists populated the boulevards. With all this pushing and shoving things didn't always proceed peaceably. Embittered quarrels arose as to who had renounced normality with the most determination, who was more out of the ordinary than anyone else. With increasing competition, standards rose. Sad to say, the compulsion to exaggerate brought a degree of hysteria in its train. The struggle of all these unique individuals was exacerbated by the appearance of umpires with stop-watches. It was no longer just a question of who was more exceptional, more militant, more extreme than the others, but also of who was quicker in his deviation, in setting himself apart. It was not *that* someone wrote a whole novel without using the letter *e*, not *that* someone crapped into a tin and got his work into the world's leading museums, that was decisive, but whether he managed to do it before his rivals. Blows were inevitably exchanged. More and more participants turned up on the avant-garde's cinder track and the din grew louder. At the same time, the persecutions grew ever briefer; to get on everyone's nerves became increasingly difficult; more and more spectators shrugged their shoulders and turned away from the contests. 'This novel is a provocation!' – 'This production is a radical attempt to break with conventional patterns of behaviour' – 'This exhibition offends the public's ways of seeing.' The public faces up to all these provocative ruptures and offences with imperturbable composure, just as it does the TV adverts which promise a completely new shower experience, driving experience, tooth-brushing experience.

However, apart from such paradoxes which are a consequence of their own success – artists by themselves would never have managed to drive normality into a corner and damage its reputation so thoroughly that for millions of people it became a stigma, a kind of social bad breath. But meanwhile quite a different set of people, who had more harmful means at their disposal than brushes or typewriters, had taken a hand. In politics, too, during the nineteenth century, people came to the fore who wanted to be right at the front of things, who loved taking risks, who wanted to show the rest, the normal, ordinary, average people what a spade is, what progress is, what liberation is, the true Germany, the historic moment, the great future, the class-less society, the white man's burden, the realm of freedom etc., etc. To achieve these things it was, however, necessary to tear the average man, this creature of habit, this dull-witted, sluggish, ordinary everyman out of his rut, and that was no easy matter. People were required who were not conformists, but outsiders, exceptional not to say supermen. For as matters stood, the idea of socialism, for example, could only be carried into the working class from outside (Lenin), and equally when the fate of Germany was at stake or the blessings of civilization had to be brought to some dark continent or other, leadership personalities were required; on his own, the herdman, the little man, the average man would never have hit on the idea.

Nothing could have been achieved without an educational dictatorship; without a certain apparatus such enormous projects had no prospect of success. It was necessary to give the course of history a helping hand, and those few who looked more than a day ahead could under no circumstances allow themselves to be squeamish in their choice of means. However, here too it became apparent that outsiderness tends towards a strange dynamic. In a short time all Europe was swarming with supermen. Millions of leadership personalities and extremists contended with one another for a place at the head of the historical cohorts, fought propaganda and street battles and attempted to make the silent majority shout along, ultimately with decreasing success.

Corporal Mollenhauer from Bad Schwalbach, civilian profession – outworker, exceptionally bad marksman and of limited use for combat duty because of asthma, during the Second World War learnt to cut hair behind the lines, always carried scissors, combs, shaving soap, razor, eau de Cologne with him. Valued by everyone, including the regimental staff officers. In June 1942 was transferred to the Kharkov area with the 29th Infantry Division, later Stalingrad. After the death of Sergeant Schäufele from Esslingen (bullet lodged in body), the only barber in the encirclement. Last haircut: General Field Marshal von Paulus on 22 January 1943. Minus 8°C in the command bunker (no fuel). Returns home 1956 after thirteen years as a prisoner of war in various camps, finally at Ufa (Bashkir Soviet Republic) where his skills were very useful to him.

1956–9 'Reconstruction'. Today Mollenhauer owns a hairdressing salon in Bad Schwalbach, managed by his son-in-law, a pharmacy and a detached house with a flat, market value 645,000 marks (encumbrances under section 1 of the property register: none). Mollenhauer votes CDU/CSU. Asked what was the most important experience in his life, he replies: 'In my life there have been no important experiences, I was lucky, that's all.'

The 'normal person' is of hardly any importance to us; I would almost say, we can delete him … The 'normal person' (the words put me in a rage) is that residue, that primary element left at the bottom of the retort after the smelting process, when whatever is valuable has evaporated.

André Gide, *Paludes*, Paris 1895

## Self-quotation II: On the Difficulties of Re-education

When it's time to liberate mankind they run to the hairdresser.
Instead of following along enthusiastically behind the vanguard
they say: it's time for a beer.
Instead of fighting for the just cause
they worry about varicose veins and measles.
At the decisive moment
they look for a letter-box or a bed.
Just before the millennium breaks out
they boil nappies.
Everything fails because of these people.
You can't do anything with them.
They're worse than a bag of fleas.
Petty bourgeois vacillation!
Consumer idiots!
Remnants of the past!
We can't kill them all, can we!
We can't go on at them every day!
Yes if it wasn't for these people
then everything would look very different.
Yes if it wasn't for these people
then it would all be over in no time.
Yes if it wasn't for these people
yes then!

*Gedichte 1955–70*, Frankfurt 1971

There is only one thing more pitiful than contempt for normality and that is to worship it. Since each of these attitudes is only the reverse of the other, it's not surprising that they usually grow on the same dungheap. The attempt to glorify normality is not only a nonsense logically – because every halo loses its shine if it becomes normal headwear; it is also a political lie which is not very convincing. Demagogues, populists, know-it-alls have always declared that ordinary folk are noble, man is good, the simple countryman unspoiled and many other similar inanities.

The normal person rarely falls for such attempts to curry favour, and he immediately sees through the cheap irony with which a prince of the spirit talks of the delights of ordinariness. The *Proletkult*, germ-free 'workers' literature' and the prints produced by socialist realism met a similar fate. It's not only the breakfast roll that's normal, but marital conflict; not only slippers, but the massacre on the evening news; not only health, but also dying in hospital; not only the rubber plant, but the assembly line; not only cosiness, but also fear and trembling.

Regional Postal Director Thalmayr's project.

In 1923 in Germany several thousand women are busy connecting long-distance telephone calls. Local calls are, by this time, already largely automated (rotary selector Strowger System). Graduate engineer Thalmayr, at that time a director of telegraphs, thirty-one, single, monthly salary 414 Rentenmarks plus local allowance, is entrusted with a study whose aim is to explore the technical possibilities and problems of automatic long-distance dialling. At the end of 1924 he installs the first experimental circuit in southern Germany at the Freising (Upper Bavaria) long-distance telephone exchange, operating between two district central exchanges, though at first still with a confidential code.

In 1957, one day before his retirement – two sons from a second marriage have meanwhile completed their studies, and as Regional Postal Director he now earns, according to the pay scale, 1,720 marks – Thalmayr opens the Cham (Upper Palatinate) district network. The latest Siemens EMD units are being brought into use. The last Bavarian local network has now been connected to the subscriber trunk-dialling system.

Thalmayr's life's work, begun at the height of the inflation, was continued through four political systems: the Weimar Republic, the Third Reich, the US Military Government, the Federal Republic of Germany. The total cost, at 1981 prices, can be estimated at approximately twenty-eight billion marks. Impediments arose as a result of the financial crisis of 1923–4, the depression of 1929–31 (emergency decrees), the armaments priorities of the Four Year Plan, 1936, and of the war economy 1939–45. Further disruptions to Thalmayr's work: allied air attacks (1942–5) and restrictions on production in the electrical engineering industry (1945–9, shortage of materials, dismantling of plant).

Thalmayr joined the Nazi Party in 1934. Political activities: none. 1941 his post placed in the reserved category. Thalmayr sabotaged the Führer's order of February 1945 to blow up his life's work. On 3 March 1945 he was arrested by the Gestapo and on 21 April 1945 liberated by American troops. Demoted to telegraph work in June of the same year because of his membership of the Nazi Party, Thalmayr could nevertheless continue his task. In 1946 he was classified as a nominal party member, and in 1952 promoted to Regional Postal Director.

After the inauguration of the Cham central exchange, the reception took place in the 'Randsberger Inn' in the presence of a State Secretary from the Ministry, Thalmayr was interviewed by a journalist from the 'Upper Palatine Messenger' [*Oberpfälzer Bote*]. The conversation turned to the historical conditions of his work. Asked how he rated the social significance of his work, Thalmayr replied: 'Everyone wants to talk on the phone.'

Every one of society's norms – of course! – has a definable social location. But no such location – I'll take bets on this – can be found for normality in general. Certainly it's always already predetermined – well, by what? By class prejudices, feelings of inferiority, projections, resentments. Well, there you are! Without such cribs we would be quite unable to say what we think is normal and what's not. But wait a minute! That hardly means that the category of normality can be reduced to class conflict. Well, perhaps category is a bit too grand. At any rate, it was quite normal for the high nobility to beat each other up, get drunk and argue about gambling debts and for our original geniuses to darn their socks after the day's work was done; while the Bavarian peasants kept to their etiquette more strictly than the king, and the revolutionary working-class movement of Germany disapproved heartily of premarital sex. It can't be helped, normality occurs in the best circles. And word that the intelligence of ordinary people is only surpassed by the ordinariness of intellectuals must have spread even in academic circles. It's just as clear, at least to the initiated, where normality can be studied in its most naked, shameless form: among those who consider themselves to be outsiders.

That is why we now rise from our seats and pronounce the following sentence in the first instance: anyone who wants to investigate the riddle of normality is condemned to look in the mirror. We quote the following from the summing up: the principle according to which normality is always in the majority is true not only in an objective but also in a subjective sense. Experience of life indicates that the validity of the 95 per cent clause can be assumed. A deviation of one-twentieth is already the height of emotion. Depending on class position, profession, age, background, gender, status and milieu you shall find in your own breast what you try in vain to ignore, to deny, to split off from yourself: reserves of normality that are boundless, inexhaustible, inescapable. Before all you unique individuals assume an injured expression we would like to say: enjoy it! As long as a remnant of *common sense* still glows within your breast, as long as you stumble through each day as a dull mass, you are not quite lost. All in all a degree of common humanity cannot be denied.

Soon after being called to the Bar, R.A. Weinert, a beginner in criminal cases, discovers that his clients – pimps, burglars, conmen, most already with a criminal record – are intent only on shortening the procedure in every possible way, regardless of a whole series of rights which the criminal code grants every prisoner on remand. 'Let's get out of here!' – even though time spent on remand is automatically deducted from the prison sentence.

*145*

Weinert can't understand it and talks to his colleague Bachmann, an old hand. 'Just imagine, Weinert, that you move into a tenement block and find out that the tenants change every few days. Never-ending commotion in the house, no idea who lives next door and who you'll meet in the lift; apart from that constant snooping by the landlord, the neighbours, the caretaker's wife, etc.'

Weinert rejoins that the comparison isn't a very good one. 'Why not? Jail is a kind of home for our clients. There are old friends, firm rules for everything, trade flourishes, enmities develop, friendships, pecking orders, favours are exchanged, cosy habits, movable feasts ... In a way once sentence has finally been passed then nothing else can happen: no more interrogations, no more uncertainty, no judge, no public prosecutor, no police. In other words you know what to expect. That's something at least! More than you think ...!'

Three strategies for normality:

1. *Silence.* It is always only minorities who speak out in public. The majority, every majority, remains silent. It is difficult, strictly speaking it's impossible, to say if it pays any attention at all to what the minority says. Does it reject everything it sees, hears and reads? Rejection would already be putting it too strongly. It's more a matter of a specialized, highly developed ability to ignore, of perceiving things 'as if', of an almost ironic inclusion and exclusion, of a silent reserve, which is ultimately unbreakable.

That, of course, grieves all those who 'have something to say', the politicians and the opinion-makers, the educationalists and publicity men, the artists and preachers. Even though the majority by and large tolerates them, feeds them and even flatters them without rebelling, they do find it disturbing that the majority ignores their pronouncements, is deaf to them. The 'dull mass' simply waves it all away. For example, it hears 'Side by side with the glorious Soviet Union', or 'The People's Computer is here!' – and replies, if at all: 'Excuse me, but first

I've got to heat up a bottle for my little Tommy.' The response to the catchwords 'mankind's dream' is: 'Maybe, but my pension ...' If someone says 'no future', or 'apocalypse', then expect the majority, after nodding politely, to change the subject and turn to the question of what's happening to Tottenham Hotspur this season.

Because this is all so damned annoying, masses of question-naires are distributed, meetings called, polls conducted: 'Would you be prepared to make sacrifices for future generations? Would you buy blue toothpaste? How many books have you read during the last year? Which position do you prefer during inter-course? Whom would you vote for if national elections were held on the coming Sunday?' Evasive phrases, laconic lies, refined forms of silence are the reply. (Last year a third of those inter-viewed by a public opinion research company willingly confirmed the popularity and high profile of a named Bonn minister who never existed.)

One can easily feel sorry for the eager opinion-makers who, day in day out, announce the trends, give out slogans, evoke the current mood, sell beliefs, create fashions, direct appeals, make predictions. Sixty-five years of manipulation, pedagogy, censor-ship, monopoly of information in the Soviet Union, the dream of every pedagogic dictatorship, and what's the result? An imper-ceptible shrug of the shoulders, a hint of resignation around the mouth, an invincible silence. This *silentium populi* is the limit of all consciousness industries, all media, all propaganda.

2. *Regression.* A liking for the garden gnome and for pinball, for skittles, disco, horoscopes and Suzuki is not, as the enlighteners believe, wilful ignorance or the systematic stupefaction of defenceless masses. No historic lag is crying out to be made up. It's the poor victims of manipulation who are silently but ener-getically refusing every kind of instruction. Not for any price do they want to be raised to a higher level of culture, of taste, of poli-tical consciousness, i.e. to where the particular spokesman of the day is standing.

The majority doesn't turn away to superstition, sport and

entertainment by mistake, because it doesn't know any better, it does so quite intentionally. Escapism is a well-defined strategy. The illusory is systematically and deliberately sought out. Regression is a staple food. *Bild* newspaper is indispensable because it is meaningless, not despite being so; for the important things we call history have always confronted us, in our capacity as majority, in only one form: as impositions.

3. *Persistence.* The good and the bad habits of normality are only for the smallest part a product of that 'system' which stands on the historical order of the day. They are above all sediments, in which for good or for bad, immeasurably old experiences have been deposited. Normality is collective memory in its most solid form, and to that extent it is always out of date. There's something disturbing in that, a scandal which must deeply embitter anyone aiming to change the world. In the mouths of those who have something to say, the word 'change' has taken on a peculiar pathos in the course of the last hundred years, as if it always stood for something desirable. The majority is not so sure about that; with its elephant's memory it has presumably understood very well that the result of the furious transformations it has experienced has often enough been catastrophic.

Its silence can also be interpreted as a delaying resistance to the dizzying speed with which the so-called lifeworld is changing. To everyone for whom uncompromising modernization is an inner need, the normality of everyday life can only be perceived as a declining remnant, as a hindrance to be planed away as quickly as possible.

This is in marked contrast to the recalcitrance of the majority, a recalcitrance which is all the more difficult to overcome as it is not rooted in an idea but functions quite materially, not to say materialistically. An obvious example can fairly easily demonstrate the doggedness with which normality pursues its goals. German Fascism can be understood as a large-scale attempt to make a clean sweep. At the end of the Second World War this experiment seemed to have succeeded: the whole country was a *tabula rasa*. That Hitler's (and Morgenthau's) calculation nevertheless did not work out was the fault of the women who cleared away the rubble, the returned prisoners of war, the Ami-girls, cellar children, black marketeers, coal thieves, allotment gardeners, denazification certificate holders, people who started building their own homes, handymen, a silent majority who insisted on reconstructing Germany.

To our social sciences, which until now have failed to colonize it, normality appears as a dark continent, an impenetrable black hole, which swallows up the light of curiosity, of criticism, of dominant rationality. Normality is a defensive power, but it is incapable of resigning. Opinions, philosophies, ideologies will never be able to get to grips with it.

In its small life – but can life ever be something small? – there are enormous reserves of labour power, cunning, readiness to help, vengefulness, stubbornness, energy, prudence, courage and savagery. Fear of the future is not its strength. If the species is capable of surviving, then it will presumably owe its persistence not to some outsiders but to quite ordinary, normal people.

*(1982)*

# 11

# Two Notes on the End of

# the World

## I

The apocalypse is part of our ideological baggage. It is aphro-
disiac, nightmare, a commodity like any other. You can call
it a metaphor for the collapse of capitalism, which as we all
known has been imminent for more than a century. We
come up against it in the most varied shapes and guises: as
warning finger and scientific forecast, collective fiction and
sectarian rallying cry, as product of the leisure industry, as
superstition, as vulgar mythology, as a riddle, a kick, a joke,
a projection. It is ever present but never 'actual': a second
reality, an image that we construct for ourselves, an incessant
product of our fantasy, the catastrophe in the mind.

All this it is and more, as one of the oldest ideas of the
human species. Thick volumes could have been written on its
origins, and of course such volumes have actually been
written. We know likewise all manner of things about its
chequered history, about its periodic ebb and flow, and the
way these fluctuations connect with the material process of
history. The idea of the apocalypse has accompanied utopian
thought since its first beginnings, pursuing it like a shadow,
like a reverse side that cannot be left behind: without catastrophe, no millennium, without apocalypse, no paradise. The
idea of the end of the world is simply a negative utopia.

But even the end of the world is no longer what it was.

The film playing in our heads, and still more uninhibitedly in our unconscious, is distinct in many respects from the dreams of old. In its traditional coinings, the apocalypse was a venerable, indeed a sacred idea. But the catastrophe which we are so concerned with (or rather haunted by) is an entirely secularized phenomenon. We read its signs on the walls of buildings, where they appear overnight, clumsily sprayed; we read them on the printouts spewed forth by the computer. Our seven-headed monster answers to many names: police state, paranoia, bureaucracy, terror, economic crisis, arms race, destruction of the environment. Its four riders look like the heroes of Westerns and sell cigarettes, while the trumpets that proclaim the end of the world serve as theme music for a commercial break. Once people saw in the apocalypse the unknowable avenging hand of God. Today it appears as the methodically calculated product of our own actions, and the spirits whom we hold responsible for its approach we call reds, oil sheikhs, terrorists, multinationals; the gnomes of Zürich and the Frankensteins of the biology labs; UFOs and neutron bombs; demons from the Kremlin or the Pentagon: an underworld of unimaginable conspiracies and machinations, whose strings are pulled by the all-powerful cretins of the secret police.

The apocalypse was also once a singular event, to be expected unannounced as a bolt from the blue: an unthinkable moment that only seers and prophets could anticipate – and, of course, no one wanted to listen to their warnings and predictions. Our end of the world, on the other hand, is sung from the rooftops even by the sparrows; the element of surprise is missing; it seems only to be a question of time. The doom we picture for ourselves is insidious and agonizingly slow in its approach, the apocalypse in slow motion. It is reminiscent of that hoary avant-garde classic of the silent cinema in which we see a gigantic factory chimney crack up and collapse noiselessly on the screen, for a full twenty minutes, while the spectators, in a kind of indolent comfort, lean back in their threadbare velvet seats and nibble their popcorn and peanuts. After the performance the futurologist mounts the stage. He looks like a poor imitation of Dr Strangelove, the mad scientist, only he is repulsively fat. Quite calmly he informs us that the atmospheric ozone layer will have disappeared in twenty years' time, so that we shall surely be· toasted by cosmic radiation if we are lucky enough to survive until then; unknown substances in our milk are driving us to psychosis; and with the rate at which world population is growing there will soon be standing room only on our planet. All this with Havana cigar in hand, in a well-composed speech of impeccable logic. The audience suppresses a yawn, even though, according to the professor, imminent disaster looms ahead. But it's not going to come this afternoon. This afternoon, everything will go on just as before, perhaps a little bit worse than last week, but not so that anyone would notice. If one or other of us should be a little depressed this afternoon, which cannot of course be ruled out, then the thought might strike him, irrespective of whether he works in the Pentagon or the underground, irons shirts or welds sheet metal, that it would really be simpler if we were rid of the problem once and for all; if the catastrophe really did *come*. However, this is out of the question. Finality, which was formerly one of the major attributes of the apocalypse, and one of the reasons for its power of attraction, is no longer granted us.

We have also lost another traditional aspect of the end of the world. Previously, it was generally agreed that the event would affect everyone simultaneously and without exception: the never-satisfied demand for equality and justice found in this conception its last refuge. But as we see it today, doom is no longer a leveller, quite the opposite. It differs from country to country, from class to class, from place to place. While it is already overtaking some, others can watch it on television. Bunkers are built, ghettos walled in, fortresses erected, body-guards hired, on a large scale as well as a small. Corresponding to the country house with burglar alarms and electric fences, we have whole countries, on the international scale, who fence themselves in while others go to ruin. The nightmare of the end of the world does not end this temporal disparity, it simply radicalizes it. Its African and Indian versions are overlooked with a shrug of the shoulders by those not directly affected – including the African and Indian governments. At this point, finally, the joke comes to an end.

## II

Berlin, Spring 1978

Dear Balthasar,

When I wrote my comment on the apocalypse – a work which I confess was not particularly thorough or serious – I was still unaware that you were also concerned with the future. You complained to me on the telephone that you were 'not really getting anywhere'. That sounded almost like an appeal for help. I know you well enough to understand your dilemma. Today it is only the technocrats who are advancing towards the year 2000 full of optimism, with the unerring instinct of lemmings, and you are not one of their number. On the contrary, you are a loyal soul, always ready to assemble under the banner of utopia. You want as much as ever to hold fast to the principle of hope. You wish us well: i.e. not only you and me, but humanity as a whole.

Please don't be angry if this sounds ironic. That isn't my fault. You wanted to see if I would come to your help. My letter will be disapppointing to you, and perhaps you even feel that I am attacking you from behind. That isn't my intention. All I would like to suggest is that we consider things with gloves off.

The strength of left-wing theory of whatever stamp, from Babeuf through to Bloch, i.e. for more than a century and a half, lay in the fact that it based itself on a positive utopia which had no peer in the existing world. Socialists, communists and anarchists all shared the conviction that their struggle would introduce the realm of freedom in a foreseeable period of time. They 'knew just where they wanted to go and just what, with the help of history, strategy and effort, they ought or needed to do to get there. Now, they no longer do.' I read these lapidary words recently in an article by the English historian Eric Hobsbawm. But this old communist does not forget to add that, 'In this respect, they do not stand alone. Capitalists are just as much at a loss as socialists to understand their future, and just as puzzled by the failure of their theorists and prophets.'

Hobsbawm is quite correct. The ideological deficit exists on both sides. Yet the loss of certainty about the future does not balance out. It is harder to bear for the Left than for those who never had any other intention but to hang on at any price to some snippet of their own power and privileges. This is why the Left, including you dear Balthasar, go in for grumbling and complaining.

No one is ready any more, you say, or in a position either, to put forward a positive idea that goes beyond the horizon of the existing state of affairs. Instead of this, false consciousness is rampant; the stage is dominated by apostasy and confusion. I remember our last conversation about the 'new irrationalism', your lamenting over the resignation that you sense on all sides, and your tirades against the flippant doomsters, shameless pessimists and apostles of defeatism. I shall be careful not to contradict you here. But I wonder whether one thing has not escaped you in all this; the fact that in these expressions and moods there is precisely what you were looking for – an idea that goes beyond the limits of our present existence. For in the last analysis, the world has certainly not come to an end (or else we could not talk about it); and so far no conclusive proof has reached me that an event of this kind is going to take place at any clearly ascertainable point in time. The conclusion I draw from this is that we are dealing here with a utopia, even if a negative one; and I further maintain that, for the historical reasons I mentioned, left-wing theory is not particularly well equipped to deal with this kind of utopia.

Your reactions are only further evidence for my assumption. The first stanza of your song, in which you bewail the prevailing intellectual situation, is promptly followed by the second, in which you enumerate the scapegoats. For such an old hand at theory as yourself, it is not difficult to lay hands on the guilty parties: the ideological opponent, the agents of anti-communism, the manipulation of the mass media. Your arguments are in no way new to me. They remind me of an essay that came to my attention a few years back. The author, an American Marxist by the name of H.C. Greisman, came to the conclusion that: 'The images of decline of which the media are so fond are designed to hypnotize and stupefy the masses in such a way that they come to see any hope of revolution as meaningless.'

What is striking in this proposition is above all its essential defensiveness. For a hundred years or so, as long as it was sure of its ground, classical Marxist theory argued the very opposite. It did not see the images of catastrophe and visions of doom of the time simply as lies concocted by some secret seducers and spread among the people, but sought rather to explain them in social terms, as symbolic depictions of a thoroughly real process. In the twenties, to take just one example, the Left saw the attraction that Spengler's historical metaphysics had for the bourgeois intelligentsia in precisely this way: *The Decline of the West* was in reality nothing more than the imminent collapse of capitalism.

Today, on the other hand, someone like yourself no longer feels his views confirmed by the apocalyptic fantasy, but instead feels threatened, reacting with last-ditch slogans and defensive gestures. To be quite frank, dear Balthasar, it seems to me that the result of these obeisances is rather wretched. I don't mean by this that it is simply false. You do not, of course, fail to resort to the well-tried path of critique of ideology. And it is child's play to show that the rise and fall of utopian and apocalyptic moods in history corresponds to the political, social and economic conditions of the time. It is also uncontestable that they are exploited politically, just like any other fantasy that exists on a mass scale.

You need not imagine you have to teach me the ABC. I know as well as you that the fantasy of doom always suggests the desire for miraculous salvation; and it is clear to me, too, that the Bonapartist saviour is always waiting in the wings, in the form of military dictatorship and right-wing putsch. When it is a question of survival, there have always been people all too ready to place their trust in a strong man. Nor do I find it surprising that those who have called for one more or less expressly in the last few years should include both a liberal and a Stalinist: the American sociologist Helibroner, and the German philosopher Harich. It is also beyond doubt that the apocalyptic metaphor promises relief from the analytical thought, as it tends to throw everything together in the same pot. From the Middle East conflict to a postal strike, from punk style to a nuclear reactor disaster, anything and everything is conceived as a hidden sign of an imaginary totality: catastrophe 'in general'. The tendency to hasty generalization damages that residual power of clear thought that we still have left. In this sense, the feeling of doom does not lead just to mystification. It goes without saying that the new irrationalism which so troubles you can in no way solve the real problems. On the contrary, it makes them appear insoluble.

This is all very easy to say, but it does not help matters all that much. You try and fight the fantasies of destruction with quotations from the classics. But these rhetorical victories, dear Balthasar, remind me of the heroic feats of Baron von Münchhausen. Like him, you want to reach your goal alone and unafraid; and to avoid departing from the correct straight line, you, too, are ready in case of need to leap on to a cannon-ball.

But the future is not a play-ground for hussars, nor is ideological criticism a cannon-ball. You should leave it to the futurologists to imitate the boastings of an old tin soldier. The future that you have in mind is in no way an object of science. It is something that exists only in the medium of social fantasy, and the organ by which it is chiefly experienced is the unconscious. Hence the power of these images that we all produce, day and night: not only with the head, but with the whole body. Our collective dreams of fear and desire weigh at least as heavy, probably heavier, than our theories and analyses.

The really threadbare character of customary ideological critique is that it ignores all this and wants to know nothing of it. Has it not struck you that it has long ceased to explain things that do not fit its schemas, and started to taboo them instead? Without our having properly noticed, it has taken on the role of an agency of adaptation. Alongside the state censorship of the law-and-order people there are now ranged the mental-hospital orderlies of the Left in the social and human sciences, who would like to pacify us with their tranquillizers. Their maxims are: (1) never concede anything; (2) reduce the unfamiliar to the familiar; (3) always think only with the head; (4) the unconscious must do what it is told.

The arrogance of these academic exorcists is surpassed only by their impotence. They fail to understand that myths cannot be refuted by seminars, and that their bans on ideas have a very short reach. What help is it to them, for example, and what use to us, if for the hundredth time they declare any comparison between natural and social processes to be inadmissible and reactionary? The elementary power of fantasy teaches millions of people to break this ban constantly. Our ideologists only raise a smile when they attempt to obliterate such ineffaceable images as flood and fire, earthquake and hurricane. Moreover, there are people in the ranks of natural scientists who are in a position to elaborate fantasies of this kind in their own fashion, and make them productive instead of banning them: mathematicians drafting a topographical theory of catastrophe, or biochemists who have ideas about certain analogies between biological and social evolution. We are still waiting in vain for the sociologist who will understand that, in a sense that is still to be decoded, there is no longer any such thing as a purely natural catastrophe.

Instead of this, our theorists, chained to the philosophical traditions of German idealism, refuse to admit even today what every bystander has long since grasped: that there is no world spirit; that we do not know the laws of history; that even the class struggle is an 'indigenous' process, which no vanguard can consciously plan and lead; that social evolution, like natural evolution, has no subject and is therefore unpredictable; that consequently, when we act politically, we never manage to achieve what we had in mind, but rather something quite different, which at one time we could not even have imagined; and that the crisis of all positive utopias has its basis precisely in this fact. The projects of the nineteenth century have been falsified completely and without exception by the history of the twentieth century. In the essay I already mentioned, Eric Hobsbawm recalls a congress held by the Spanish anarchists in 1898. They sketched a glorious picture of life after the victory of the revolution: a world of tall shining buildings with elevators that would save climbing stairs, electric light for all, garbage-disposers and marvellous household gadgets ... This vision of humanity, presented with Messianic pathos, now looks strikingly familiar: in many parts of our cities it has already become reality. There are victories that are hard to distinguish from defeats. No one feels comfortable in recalling the promise of the October Revolution sixty years ago: once the capitalists were driven out of Russia, a bright future without exploitation and oppression would dawn for the workers and peasants ...

Are you still with me, Balthasar? Are you still listening? I have come to the end of my letter. Forgive me if it has got rather long, and if my sentences have taken on a mocking undertone. It's not me who injected this, it's a kind of objective, historic mockery, and the laugh, for better or worse, is always on the losing side. We all have to bear it together.

Optimism and pessimism, my dear friend, are so much sticking-plaster for fortune-tellers and the writers of leading articles. The pictures of the future that humanity draws for itself, both positive and negative utopias, have never been unambiguous. The idea of the millennium, the sunshine state, was not the pallid dream of a land of milk and honey; it always had its elements of fear, panic, terror and destruction. And the apocalyptic fantasy, conversely, produces more than just pictures of decadence and despair: it also contains, inescapably bound up with the terror, the demand for vengeance, for justice, impulses of relief and hope.

The Pharisees, those who always know best, want to convince us that the world would be all right again if the 'progressive forces' took a strong line with people's fantasies; if they themselves were only sitting on the Central Committee, and pictures of doom could be prohibited by decree of the Party. They refuse to understand that it is we ourselves who produce these pictures, and that we hold on to them because they correspond to our experiences, desires and fears: on the motorway between Frankfurt and Bonn, in front of the TV screen that shows we are at war, beneath helicopters, in the corridors of clinics, employment offices and prisons – because, in a single word, they are in this sense realistic.

I scarcely need reassure you, dear Balthasar, that I know as little of the future as you do yourself. I am writing to you because I do not count you among the pigeon-holers and ticket-punchers of the world spirit. What I wish you, as I wish myself and us all, is a little more clarity about our own confusion, a little less fear of our own fear, and a little more attention, respect and modesty in the face of the unknown. Then we shall be able to see a little further.

Yours, H.M.E.

*(1978)*

Printed in the United States
by Baker & Taylor Publisher Services